AN EDGAR ALLAN POE COMPANION

Other books by J. R. Hammond
H. G. WELLS: AN ANNOTATED BIBLIOGRAPHY OF HIS WORKS
AN H. G. WELLS COMPANION
H. G. WELLS: INTERVIEWS AND RECOLLECTIONS (*editor*)

Frontispiece Edgar Allan Poe, *circa* 1840, from a contemporary portrait by Matthew Brady

AN EDGAR ALLAN POE COMPANION

A guide to the short stories,
romances and essays

J. R. HAMMOND

BARNES & NOBLE BOOKS
TOTOWA, NEW JERSEY

Buffalo
June,
1983

© J. R. Hammond 1981

First Published in the U.S.A. 1981 by
BARNES & NOBLE BOOKS
81, Adams Drive, Totowa,
New Jersey, 07512
ISBN 0–389–20172–3

Printed in Hong Kong

Poe's tales, imperfect as they are, provide a case-study in the development of the Western literary imagination
                                      KENNETH GRAHAM

My life has been *whim* – impulse – passion – a longing for solitude – a scorn of all things present, in an earnest desire for the future
                                      EDGAR ALLAN POE

It is remarkable that, whatever the tribulations of his private life, Poe never lost his vision of his artistic destiny or his essential seriousness
                                      GEOFFREY RANS

The story of Edgar Allan Poe is one of the great tragedies of literature
                                      DAVID SINCLAIR

Contents

List of Plates and Map	ix
Preface	xi
PART I	1
The Life of Edgar Allan Poe	3
Poe's Literary Reputation	25
PART II AN EDGAR ALLAN POE DICTIONARY	35
PART III THE SHORT STORIES	59
PART IV THE ROMANCES	113
PART V ESSAYS AND CRITICISM	133
PART VI THE POETRY	149
PART VII CHARACTERS AND LOCATIONS IN POE'S FICTION	167
Appendix – Film Versions	189
References	193
Select Bibliography	196
Index	202

List of Plates and Map

Frontispiece
Edgar Allan Poe, *circa* 1840
1 Manor House School, Stoke Newington
2 Rear view of Manor House School
3 The mother of Edgar Allan Poe
4 The house in which 'The Raven' was finished
5 Title page of *Tamerlane*
6 Virginia Poe, *née* Clemm
7 Facsimile of verses by Poe
8 Poe's cottage at Fordham
9 Poe in the closing years of his life

Map Stoke Newington, London, *circa* 1820   8

For the provision of illustrations, and permission to reproduce them, grateful acknowledgements are made to: Hackney Library Services, London Borough of Hackney (frontispiece, 1, 2, and map); BBC Hulton Picture Library (3 and 4).

Preface

The present work stems from an interest in Edgar Allan Poe extending over thirty years. Ever since, as a schoolboy, I first acquired a copy of *Tales of Mystery and Imagination* and came under the spell of those unforgettable short stories I have been deeply impressed with Poe as a literary artist and have felt a sense of debt to him which I hope this *Companion* can in some measure repay.

The *Companion* is intended to serve as a guide to the whole range of his work – including the short stories, the poetry and the criticism – and to enable the reader to read and enjoy Poe with a keener appreciation. I have found that as work on the book proceeded my own fascination with Poe as a man and as a writer has intensified, and I found myself being drawn more and more towards a closer scrutiny of this most intriguing of literary figures. I trust that I have succeeded in conveying to the reader something of my own enthusiasm for his writings.

I have found it extraordinarily difficult in practice to present a balanced and detached view of Poe as an individual. So much has been written about him since his death – some of it adulatory, some of it hypercritical – that anyone seeking to present a dispassionate appraisal has to steer his way through a labyrinth of critical and biographical works in an attempt to arrive at a balanced assessment. The reader must judge the extent to which I have succeeded in the pages which follow. But I start from the conviction that he was a literary craftsman of very considerable importance and that his significance to the twentieth century is only now beginning to be appreciated.

I am indebted in particular to the following critical works: *Israfel: The Life and Times of Edgar Allan Poe* by Hervey Allen,

Edgar Allan Poe by David Sinclair, *Poe: A Biography* by William Bittner, and *The Portable Edgar Allan Poe* edited by Philip Van Doren Stern. These four works have been constantly at my side throughout the writing of this *Companion* and, amidst so much about Poe of an ephemeral or uncritical nature, I am indebted to the authors concerned for their reliability and balance. Other sources of reference and Poe scholarship will be found listed in the Select Bibliography.

The basic text of Poe's works used throughout this book is that of *The Complete Works of Edgar Allan Poe*, edited by James A. Harrison, and the extracts are printed by kind permission of Harper and Row, Publishers, Inc., New York. The extracts from the works of H. G. Wells are reproduced by permission of the Executors of the Wells Estate. The quotation by Kenneth Graham is taken from the Preface to *Selected Tales of Edgar Allan Poe*, and is reproduced by permission of Oxford University Press. J. M. Dent & Sons Ltd. kindly gave permission to quote material from *Edgar Allan Poe* by David Sinclair.

I wish to place on record my warm thanks to the Stoke Newington District Library (London Borough of Hackney) for so generously permitting unrestricted access to their Edgar Allan Poe Collection. The courtesy and helpfulness of the library staff, in particular Miss J. L. Dailey, the District Reference Librarian, have been of invaluable assistance in my researches. I also wish to acknowledge my thanks to the following: Miss Julia Tame, for her encouragement and helpfulness on behalf of the publishers; Mrs. M. Squires, for her patience and skill in typing the manuscript; my brother, Mr. Edward Hammond, for introducing me to Poe's writings many years ago; and Mr. Joe Wharton, my former teacher at Peoples College, Nottingham, for first kindling my enthusiasm for English literature. Lastly I thank my wife for her forbearance during the many silent hours I spent writing.

J. R. HAMMOND

Part I

The Life of Edgar Allan Poe

In May 1827 the nineteen-year-old proprietor of a little printing shop at 70 Washington Street, Boston, U.S.A., issued a small booklet entitled *Tamerlane and Other Poems* 'By a Bostonian'. The booklet, bound in yellow tea-tinted paper covers, consisted of forty pages and contained eleven poems by an unknown author. The printer, Calvin F. S. Thomas, has since faded into obscurity – his sole title to fame being his name upon the title-page of this modest publication. Its author, on the other hand, has since become world famous as one of the greatest American writers and as one of the most potent influences on English and European literature.

How did it come about that an obscure pamphlet issued by a jobbing printer has since become one of the rarest items of Americana – so rare indeed that only four genuine copies are now known to exist? How is it that this short collection of poems of which only forty or fifty copies were printed and which attracted not a single review (although it was *mentioned* in two literary journals) now occupies an honoured place in the history of our literature? Most important of all, how did it come about that its eighteen-year-old author, who was then penniless and completely unknown, is now renowned not only as a poet but as a pioneer of science fiction and of the detective story, and as the undisputed master of horror and mystery? To answer these questions we will need to trace the story of his life from their humble beginnings in that same city of Boston.

* * * * *

Edgar Poe was born at 62 Carver Street, Boston, on 19 January 1809. His father, David Poe, who rented the wooden house in which his son was born, was an actor. He was of Scotch-Irish ancestry and his forbears can be traced back to tenant farmers in County Cavan, Ireland. His father, also named David Poe, a native of Pennsylvania, settled in Baltimore and had a varied career which included furniture-making and serving as Assistant Deputy Quartermaster of the Baltimore Company of the Revolutionary Army. David Poe the actor was born in 1784. At the age of eighteen, having become keenly interested in amateur theatricals, he abandoned a career in law to pursue the roving life of a theatrical player. He seems to have been a man of romantic disposition, with a gentlemanly charm, but with a self-consciousness which denied him success in any but the most minor acting roles. He was also delicate and suffered intermittently from tuberculosis. He never achieved fame as an actor, in sharp contrast to his actress wife whom he had married in April 1806.

Elizabeth Arnold Hopkins, the daughter of London theatrical parents, was English. She was born Elizabeth Arnold but was the widow of an American actor named Hopkins who had died in 1805. After her marriage to David Poe the couple continued to appear on the stage in touring theatrical companies, appearing in Philadelphia, New York and Boston. There were three children born of this union, William Henry Leonard Poe (born in 1807 and died of tuberculosis in 1831), Edgar, and Rosalie (born 10 December 1810 [?]). Their life together must have been a continual struggle against poverty and ill health, despite the fact that Elizabeth was an accomplished actress, dancer and singer whose performances received enthusiastic reviews. They succeeded in earning a bare living until the summer of 1810, when David Poe disappeared without trace. What became of him after this date is not known. Whether he abandoned his wife in favour of another woman, or, weary of the struggle against penury, left to seek a new life elsewhere is uncertain. Tradition has it that he died in Virginia in October 1810, but this has not been substantiated.

Elizabeth, deprived of her husband and with a young family to support, left New York and travelled south to Richmond, where she was already well known. She was accompanied by the child Edgar, William Henry having been left with his grandparents in Baltimore. Tragically, Elizabeth Poe was now dying of consumption. She continued to appear on the stage in Richmond and Norfolk, dancing and singing, and resumed this career even after the birth of her daughter Rosalie. She died in Richmond on 8 December 1811, having lived her final months in conditions of crushing poverty and illness, despite the efforts of kind friends to help her. Among the group of sympathetic and well-meaning ladies who had helped to look after Mrs. Poe during her last illness were a Mrs. Frances Allan and a Mrs. William Mackenzie. Mrs. Mackenzie and her husband decided to adopt the infant Rosalie; Mrs. Allan and her husband John, who were childless, adopted the boy Edgar.

Frances Keeling Valentine Allan was then a charming and attractive young woman of twenty-seven. Her husband, John Allan, was a native of Irvine, Scotland, where he had been born in 1780. He had emigrated from Scotland to Richmond whilst still a young man and had set up in business as a merchant, trading in tobacco, grain and flour, tea, coffee and wines. Frances was clearly very much attached to the attractive and romantic-looking Edgar and John Allan fell in with her wishes that he should be brought up as if he were their own son, although legal adoption formalities were never completed – this was by no means unusual by the standards of the time. At the age of four Edgar was sent to a dame school in Richmond and then to a boys' school run by a Mr. William Ewing. Ewing remarked later that Poe was 'a charming boy', and was evidently impressed with his liking for lessons and his interest in books. Edgar, then, received the finest start in life the Allans could secure for him and seemed destined to become in all respects their adopted son. That his circumstances in later life did not fulfil the promise of his early years is one of the tragedies of Edgar Allan Poe.

By 1815 John Allan's business interests were expanding and with the ending of the Second War of Independence (and the ending therefore of hostilities between Britain and the United States) the time seemed favourable for a visit to England and Scotland in order to develop his enterprise in Britain. For Allan too such a visit was a welcome opportunity to enjoy a reunion with relatives and friends in his native land. In June 1815 Allan set sail for England, accompanied by his wife, his sister-in-law Miss Valentine, and Edgar. After a five-week journey from Norfolk to Liverpool the family travelled to Irvine in Ayrshire where, during the summer of 1815, the six-year-old Edgar attended the local academy, no doubt in company with his Allan 'cousins'. Irvine at that time was a picturesque seaport surrounded by beautiful, romantic countryside – in the strangest contrast to the scenery he had known in Virginia – and this rainswept terrain, rich in ancient ruins and winding rivers, must have made a deep impression on his mind.

In the autumn of that year the family returned to England (this journey also involved a sea voyage for part of the way and Edgar, fascinated as always by the sea, would have stored many mental impressions of the experience) arriving in London in early October. Poe seems to have remained in London with the Allans until the end of 1815, when he returned to Irvine to attend the grammar school once more. In the following year Allan decided to send him to a boarding school at 16 Sloane Street, Chelsea, where he remained until the spring of 1817. Little is known of the tuition he received at this school although a bill has survived which reveals that 'Master Allan' studied, among other subjects, writing, spelling, geography, the church catechism and English history.

Meanwhile Allan had worries on his mind. His business was not flourishing as well as he had hoped – 1817 proved to be a poor year for trade, with fluctuating prices, heavy taxation and widespread unemployment. It was proving far more difficult and expensive to establish a London branch than he had anticipated, and his wife's health had markedly deteriorated since their arrival in Britain. Worried and distracted, he sought some means of securing a good education for Edgar so that he could devote his time and energies wholly to his business interests. He found the school he sought in the Manor House School at Stoke Newington; now a suburb of London but then a small village with an identity of its own. This school, under its headmaster, the Reverend John Bransby, was an exclusive academy for young gentlemen, and here Poe was to remain from the autumn of 1817 until May 1820.

There can be no question that the two years and more which Poe spent at Stoke Newington exercised a profound influence on his imagination and outlook. Not only did it yield one of his most fascinating short stories, 'William Wilson', but it brought him into direct association with a culture older by far than any he had yet experienced. The school buildings themselves were not old (the academy was a plain Georgian house standing on the north-east corner of Church Street and what is now Edwards Lane) but close by stood the Manor House itself, an Elizabethan mansion steeped in centuries of history, and all around stood gracious eighteenth-century houses in shady squares and lanes. Reflecting on the experience many years later in 'William Wilson' he wrote:

> At this moment I feel the refreshing chilliness of its deeply-shadowed avenues, inhale the fragrance of its thousand shrubberies, and thrill anew with indefinable delight, at the deep, hollow note of the churchbell, breaking, each hour, with sudden and sullen roar, upon the stillness of the dusky atmosphere in which the fretted Gothic steeple lay imbedded and asleep.

It should be noted in passing that the headmaster described in 'William Wilson' bears no resemblance to the actual John Bransby, although Poe gives him the same name. In real life Bransby was a convivial man with a love of field sports; he was a classical scholar with an enthusiasm for natural history and seems to have been held in high esteem by his scholars. He wrote afterwards that he found Poe 'intelligent, wayward, and wilful', and indeed it is not difficult to believe that the proud young Edgar, with his American accent and un-English ways, his love of reading and precious manner, must have made a somewhat priggish impression on both staff and pupils. He did well at his lessons, excelling particularly in history and literature, and Allan could rightly be proud of him. (Allan wrote to a friend in March 1818: 'Edgar is a fine boy and I have no reason to complain of his progress.') But by the spring of 1820 Allan's business ventures were in serious difficulties and he determined to cut his losses and return to the United States. Depressed and heavily in debt, he withdrew Edgar from Stoke Newington and the family prepared once more to embark. In June they sailed from Liverpool to New York, arriving after a thirty-six day journey on 21 July. Edgar had entered England a shy and introspective boy of six; he left it a

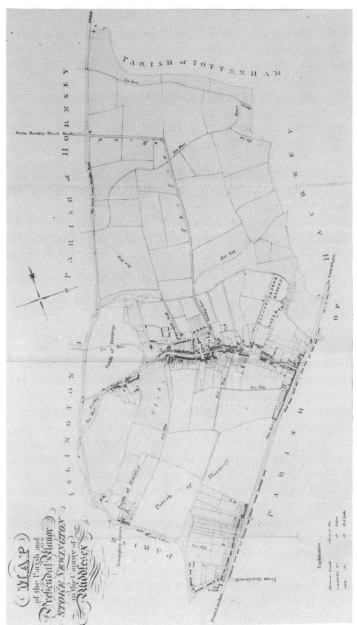

Map of Stoke Newington, *circa* 1820, from Robinson's *History and Antiquities of the Parish of Stoke Newington*. In Poe's day this was a remote, secluded village 'where were a vast number of gigantic and gnarled trees, and where all the houses were excessively ancient. In truth, it was a dream-like and spirit-soothing place, that venerable old town'.

much more self-assured boy of eleven. He gained from those five years a rich fund of memories and impressions which were to stand him in good stead in the years to come. He gained moreover a widening of his experience and understanding which proved of incalculable importance to him as a creative writer.

On returning to Richmond Allan enrolled his foster son in the school of Joseph Clarke, a fiery and pedantic Irishman of Trinity College, Dublin. Here, throughout 1821 to 1824, Edgar continued his education, studying Latin, French, classics and English literature. During these years he made his first attempts at the writing of poetry, even producing, according to Joseph Clarke, a complete manuscript volume of verses of his own composition. It was also during these years that he underwent his first experience of adolescent love when he met Jane Stith Stanard, the mother of his best friend Robert Stanard. This lady possessed a grace and classical beauty which Edgar immediately found captivating and he recognised in her the mother-figure he had sought for so long. He visited her home frequently and she seems to have encouraged his literary aspirations. The idyll was short-lived, however, for she died of a brain tumour in April 1824, aged thirty-one. The effect of her death on the sensitive youth can only be imagined; he was utterly heartbroken and idealised her as the epitomisation of transient, corruptible beauty. This obsession with the idea of the impermanence of beauty bore fruit years later in such tales as 'Berenice' and 'Morella': it was to be one of the most characteristic *leit-motifs* of his work. The immediate effect of the death of Jane Stanard was to inspire the poem 'To Helen', which is universally acknowledged as one of his most beautiful and heartfelt compositions.

Poe at this time was experiencing the rapid physical and mental changes which are characteristic of adolescence. Always inclined to be a leader in and out of school, he was now reading widely, going for long, solitary walks, and indulging in the normal escapades of a healthy boyhood. He was a powerful swimmer and became a lieutenant in the Richmond Junior Riflemen Volunteers. A friend wrote of him: 'He was very beautiful, yet brave and manly for one so young. No boy ever had a greater influence over me than he had. He was indeed a leader among his playmates.'[1]

During 1823–4 John Allan's economic fortunes continued to decline until he had reached the stage when he was all but ruined. By the spring of 1825, however, his circumstances were transformed by the inheritance of a substantial legacy from his uncle, William Galt. Allan was suddenly one of the wealthiest men in Richmond and at once moved to a larger and more handsome house. Edgar was removed from the Richmond academy and was privately tutored to enter the new University of Virginia early the following year. With the changed fortunes of his guardian he was to receive an education befitting the son of a Virginia gentleman.

He entered the University in February 1826 and remained there for one full term, leaving in December of the same year. This was a year of crucial importance for Poe. The University itself, built in classical style on spacious lawns, and the surrounding countryside of Charlottesville and the Ragged Mountains – the setting, years later, of one of his most ingenious short stories – made a deep impression on the seventeen-year-old Edgar. He must also have felt a sense of liberation at the widening opportunities which appeared to be opening out before him and the newly found friendships with wealthy young men. However, he quickly found himself in financial difficulties. Partly through his own indiscretion – he was unwise enough to contract a number of gambling debts, and then seek to recoup his debts by further gambling; and partly because of Allan's parsimony – his guardian seems to have starved him of funds throughout his stay at the University – he soon accumulated considerable debts, which Allan not unnaturally refused to pay. Poe regarded them as 'debts of honour' which as a gentleman he must repay. To Allan they were simply evidence of his adopted son's foolishness. This led to a bitter quarrel between the two, culminating in Allan's decision that Edgar could not return to the University.

John Allan exercised a profound influence on Poe's life and attitudes and it is worth digressing at this point to examine the uneasy relationship between these two totally dissimilar men. Seen from Poe's point of view it must have seemed that Allan betrayed him. Brought up as Allan's adopted son, in the full expectation that he would one day inherit some of his guardian's wealth, it seemed to Poe that Allan first of all humiliated him by deliberately starving him of money, then cut him off by leaving him nothing. To Poe, then, Allan was a hard-headed business man who was completely indifferent to his adopted son's literary aspirations and who did all he could to stifle and disown him. To Allan, not unnaturally, the situation was seen with very different eyes. Poe was, after all, no relation of his whatsoever: the boy was simply the son of strolling play actors whom he and his wife had taken pity upon out of human kindness. He had given the boy the finest education money could buy – the education, in fact, of a gentleman – in the expectation that Edgar would one day show some desire and aptitude to enter the family business. Instead, the boy seemed to have no interest in anything but the writing of poetry. It is hardly surprising that from Allan's point of view Poe seemed to be an ungrateful dilettante who was everlastingly plaguing him with begging letters. The truth is that Poe and Allan were opposites, diametrically opposed in philosophy, temperament and outlook. Where Allan was obstinate, unemotional and practical, Poe was impulsive, passionate and romantic; where Allan inhabited the world of commerce and hard economic realities Poe was most at home in the world of the poetic imagination. Faced with such a fundamental divergence of personalities it is hardly surprising that the relationship between the two became increasingly subject to disagreements and misunderstandings. Neither Poe nor Allan was wholly right or wholly wrong; each acted throughout in accordance with his deeply held beliefs. Allan's misfortune was to have taken as his adopted son a boy so totally out of sympathy, by inclination and temperament, with all that he stood for; Poe's misfortune was to have experienced as the most important formative influence of his life a man unable to comprehend his imaginative world.

The tension between the two continued for some months, culminating in an argument during which the pent-up emotions of both were released. Poe finally fled the house and put up at a tavern in Richmond, from where he wrote at once an impassioned letter to his foster father:

Sir,
After my treatment on yesterday [*sic*] and what passed between us this morning, I can hardly think you will be

surprised at the contents of this letter. My determination is
at length taken to leave your house and endeavour to find
some place in this wide world, where I will be treated – not
as you have treated me. This is not a hurried determination,
but one on which I have long considered – and having so
considered my resolution is unalterable.[2]

He went on to list his grievances, ending in a plea for his
trunk containing his clothes and books to be sent on to a
forwarding address, together with sufficient money to enable
him to travel north, where he hoped to support himself and in
time return to the University. This deliberate decision to
break with Allan and henceforth make his own way in the
world was the decisive turning point in Poe's life.

Allan replied coldly to this letter, but failed to do as Poe had
asked. He did not reply to another letter he received from Poe
on the following day which ended with the words 'I have not
one cent in the world to provide any food'. Somehow Edgar
managed to find food and lodging for the next few weeks and,
aided possibly by money sent him by Mrs. Allan (who had
always been kindly disposed towards him), he sailed for
Boston in search of a new life. His choice of Boston as a
destination may have been influenced by his mother's dying
injunction to 'cherish the city of his birth', and also by the fact
that the city was an acknowledged centre of literary activities;
he may have felt that for that reason his projected book of
poems stood a better chance of being noticed if it appeared in
Boston than if it was published in Richmond. It was during his
stay in Boston as an unknown and penniless outcast that he
made the acquaintance of a young printer, Calvin Thomas,
who undertook to print his slim volume *Tamerlane and Other
Poems*. Despite the words 'By a Bostonian', however, it must
always be borne in mind that Poe was only a Bostonian in the
sense that he happened to be *born* there. He had in fact spent
only the first few months of his life there; by education and
background he was a *Virginian*, and Richmond remained all
his life his real home.

The publication of his first volume of poetry must have
been an exciting event for him, but it brought him no money.
His resources were now at an end, and, as all appeals to Allan
had proved fruitless, he felt he had no alternative but to enlist

in the army. He took this step on 26 May 1827, enlisting for a five-year period in the United States Army under the assumed name Edgar A. Perry.

After a period of initial training at Fort Independence, Boston, he sailed in November to Charleston, Carolina, where his battery undertook garrison duty at Fort Moultrie on Sullivan's Island until December 1828. This district, with its sub-tropical fauna and flora, so utterly different from any scenery he had seen either in America or Britain, fascinated Poe and forms the background to one of his best-known tales, 'The Gold-Bug'. On the lonely beaches and scrub forests of Sullivan's Island he spent many hours wandering in search of shells and insects, for he had ample leisure and was intrigued by the island and its legends of pirates and buried treasure. Here too he continued to experiment with the writing of poetry, for he had already determined to augment his first volume with other verses. Now he wrote 'Sonnet – To Science' and the first draft of a much longer poem, 'Al Aaraaf'. Under the influence of Coleridge and Keats he was feeling his way towards a more mature, less flamboyant style, for he was now reading voraciously not only in the classics and English poets but also in European and Norse literature. His reading also included modern works such as the *Lalla Rookh* of Thomas Moore.

During his year of army service at Fort Moultrie he had abundant opportunity for reflection and seems to have become more determined than ever to pursue a literary career. Becoming disenchanted with army life, he wrote to his guardian (in December 1828) seeking his help in securing release from military service. Apparently all that was required to effect Poe's discharge was a reconciliation. Allan replied through an intermediary that he was quite content for Poe to remain where he was. Poe continued to plead with Allan, but to no avail; meanwhile he was promoted to sergeant-major, the highest non-commissioned rank in the army.

Events were now taken out of his hands, for on 28 February 1829 Frances Allan died. Before her death she extracted a solemn promise from her husband that he would not abandon Poe. Allan, grief-stricken, notified Poe of her death and he was granted ten days leave, arriving in Richmond the day after her funeral. For Poe, visiting the cemetery where both his foster mother and Jane Stanard lay buried, the event must have been traumatic; he is said to have collapsed, exhausted, on Frances Allan's grave. Gentle and affectionate, she had been one of the few people he had encountered in life who had shown him any kindness, and had on a number of occasions interceded with her husband on behalf of her adopted son. During their few days together Allan seems to have treated Poe like a prodigal son: he provided him with a black suit, presented him with fifty dollars, and discussed the possibility of securing an appointment for him to the Military Academy at West Point.

The idea of moving to West Point was apparently a compromise between their respective viewpoints: Allan was totally opposed to the idea of helping Poe to be discharged from the army in order to pursue a literary career; Poe was equally determined not to pursue a career in commerce or the law. West Point therefore represented a compromise; Poe felt that if he acquiesced with his guardian's wishes and did well at the Academy, as he had done at Fort Moultrie, there was a real chance that in time a lasting reconciliation could be achieved. While waiting for his application to the Military Academy to be processed, Poe, having been honourably discharged from the army, visited his family at Baltimore. Living there in a two-storey house were Mrs. David Poe (his grandmother), William Henry Leonard Poe (his brother), Mrs. Maria Clemm, his aunt, and her son and daughter, Henry and Virginia. Maria Clemm was the sister of Edgar's father and the widow of one William Clemm, who had died nine years after marrying her. She had then been left penniless to bring up her two children as best as she could. This was an overcrowded household struggling against poverty and ill-health; Grandmother Poe was bedridden and Edgar's brother was slowly dying of tuberculosis and alcoholism. Nevertheless, Maria Clemm was a remarkable woman and succeeded in holding the home together through a combination of hard work and charity. Edgar was immediately attracted by the Clemm-Poe menage and either then or shortly afterwards decided to join forces with them. Maria Clemm made him welcome and mothered him as if he was her own son.

In December of that year he succeeded in placing a volume of poetry, *Al Aaraaf, Tamerlane and Minor Poems* with a

Baltimore publisher, Hatch and Dunning. This contained, in addition to 'Al Aaraaf' – a long poem in which he attempted to present his philosophy of beauty in the form of an allegory – a thoroughly revised and improved version of 'Tamerlane' and a collection of other verses on which he had been working sporadically for some time. Five hundred copies of the book were printed, of which 250 were given to Poe for distribution to friends and reviewers. This was the only payment he received for this work. He was almost twenty-one years of age and already had two published works to his credit.

From June 1830 to February 1831 he served at the United States Military Academy at West Point (situated on the Hudson River above New York). Although he excelled there in both his practical and academic disciplines he was apparently unhappy and becoming increasingly disillusioned with the idea of a military career. Conversely, the prospect of devoting his life to literature was one which was becoming more and more attractive. While at West Point he continued to work at his poetry and to plan ways and means of publishing further collections of his work. While there he also began to seek refuge from his unhappiness in alcohol. Poe was one of those unfortunate people upon whom alcohol, even in the smallest quantities, has a debilitating effect. The consumption of a glass or two of wine or brandy was sufficient to produce in him symptoms of drunkenness, even of temporary oblivion. After his death this fact was seized upon by his detractors as evidence of his incurable alcoholism. It is evidence rather of the poisonous effect which all forms of drink exercised on his system: total abstinence was the only remedy for one in his condition.

During his sojourn at West Point Poe seems to have realised once and for all that the prospect of achieving a permanent reconcilation and understanding with his guardian was increasingly remote. Allan had in the meantime remarried and, since there now seemed every possibility that he and his new wife would in time have a family of their own, this inevitably lessened Edgar's chances of inheriting anything in the event of Allan's death. Reflecting on this, Edgar determined to resign from the Military Academy and henceforth to earn his living by his pen. He wrote to Allan requesting permission to resign, and indicated that if permission was not granted he would deliberately neglect his duties so that he would be dismissed. Without waiting for a reply – which in the event was not forthcoming – he began at once to neglect his parades and academic duties. He had unwittingly antagonised his guardian in a disagreement over money and Allan, still furious with him over his apparent irresponsibility, refused to help him further. The result was inevitable: Edgar was court-martialled and dismissed. He wearily made his way to Baltimore via New York and rejoined his aunt and her pathetic household. From this point onwards he regarded Maria Clemm as his mother and the destinies of himself and her household were inseparably intertwined.

Throughout 1831 and 1832 he worked steadily at the writing of poems and short stories. *Poems by Edgar A. Poe, Second Edition* was published by Elam Bliss of New York in March 1831. This was an expanded version of his 1829 collection, prefaced by a critical introduction headed 'Letter to B———' [Elam Bliss]. This essay occupies an important place in his work as a contribution to the theoretical criticism of poetry written at an early stage in his literary career. In 1832 the *Philadelphia Saturday Courier* published no fewer than five of his short stories: 'Metzengerstein', 'The Duke de L'Omelette', 'A Bargain Lost', 'Loss of Breath' and 'A Tale of Jerusalem.' Each of these, with the exception of 'Metzengerstein', is a satire on contemporary literary taste and contains little evidence of artistic promise. 'Metzengerstein' – the first of Poe's tales actually to be published (January 1832) – is a much more significant development and contains many indications of the mature Poe. The publication of this story also reveals that he was beginning to try his hand at the writing of prose as distinct from poetry and that he was experimenting with the Gothic horror story as a literary genre.

In July 1833 an event occurred which was to exercise a profound effect on Poe's subsequent career and help to channel his energies and imagination much more forcibly in the direction for which he was best fitted. The *Baltimore Saturday Visitor* announced a prize of fifty dollars for the best short story submitted by a specified date. Poe decided to enter, submitting several short stories in his meticulously neat handwriting. When the results were announced in October, he learned that 'MS. Found in a Bottle' had been awarded first prize. Not only did this mean a windfall of sorely-needed money to the Clemm-Poe family, but also the consequent publicity earned for him a considerable local renown and gained him a number of influential friends, most notably the novelist John Pendleton Kennedy. Shortly after the results were announced, Poe called on the judges to thank them personally for their commendation of his work. One of them, J. H. B. Latrobe, recalled later his impressions of the young author:

I was seated at my desk on the Monday following the publication of the tale, when a gentleman entered and introduced himself as the writer, saying that he came to thank me as one of the committee, for the award in his favour. Of this interview, the only one I ever had with Mr. Poe, my recollection is very distinct, indeed, – He was if anything, below the middle size, and yet could not be described as a small man. His figure was remarkably good, and he carried himself erect and well, as one who had been trained to it. He was dressed in black, and his frock coat was buttoned to the throat, where it met the black stock, then almost universally worn. Not a particle of white was visible. Coat, hat, boots and gloves had evidently seen their best days, but so far as mending and brushing go, everything had been done apparently, to make them presentable. On most men his clothes would have looked shabby and seedy, but there was something about this man that prevented one from criticizing his garments, and the details I have mentioned were only recalled afterwards. The impression made, however, was that the award in Mr. Poe's favour was not inopportune. *Gentleman* was written all over him. His manner was easy and quiet, and although he came to return thanks for what he regarded as deserving them, there was nothing obsequious in what he said or did. His features I am unable to describe in detail. His forehead was high, and remarkable for the great development at the temple. This was the characteristic of his head, which you noticed at once, and which I have never forgotten. The expression of his face was grave, almost sad, except when he became engaged in conversation, when it became animated and changeable. His voice I remember was very pleasing in its tone and well modulated, almost rhythmical, and his words were well chosen and unhesitating . . .

In March 1834 John Allan died in Richmond, leaving Poe nothing. His will made careful provision for his legitimate and illegitimate children but made no mention of his adopted son. From now onwards, Poe realised, he would have to earn his livelihood through his own efforts, and he began to seek a regular market for his work.

It was his newly found friend, John P. Kennedy, who recommended Poe to Thomas White, the proprietor of the recently established *Southern Literary Messenger*. During 1835 the *Messenger* published several of his tales and in August he travelled to Richmond to take up the post of assistant editor of the paper, a post he held until January 1837. Although he was nominally 'assistant' editor, in practice he carried out all the editorial functions, selecting and arranging material, handling correspondence, writing book reviews, and attending to all the detailed day to day work of the journal. The *Messenger* prospered under his editorship and soon became one of the outstanding literary magazines in the United States. In his reviews he developed his astute critical abilities, discussing the work of some of the leading novelists and poets of the day; unfortunately his astringent comments earned him enemies as well as friends in literary circles. For his editorial work he was paid a salary of ten dollars a week, rising after a time to fifteen dollars. This was extremely low pay by the standards of the time. (It is interesting to compare Poe's circumstances with those of his contemporary Charles Dickens, who was at this same time at the beginning of his literary career in London. As a reporter on the *Morning Chronicle* – a post entailing less responsibility than Poe's – Dickens was paid a salary of five guineas per week. He received £150 for the copyright of his first book, *Sketches by Boz* (1836) and an advance of thirty guineas on *Pickwick Papers* before any of the latter had been written. Had Allan's business enterprises in Britain prospered, Poe would have remained in England and received his apprenticeship as a writer in the much more favourable literary climate of London. As it was, he sought to establish himself as a writer in the very different conditions then prevailing in America.)

Meanwhile Maria Clemm and her daughter Virginia joined Poe in Richmond. He had always been attracted towards his cousin Virginia and married her in May 1836: she was then almost fourteen years of age. There has been much speculation by biographers regarding the relationship between Poe and his child-wife. That he was deeply devoted towards her there can be no doubt, but controversy persists as to whether he regarded her as a dearly-loved sister or as a wife in the conventional sense. Certainly his marriage to Virginia satisfied some deep emotional need in his makeup which found expression in some of his most finely written stories – especially such tales as 'Eleonora' and 'Berenice'.

At the beginning of 1837 he left the *Messenger* and moved with his family to New York. The literary and economic climate was unfavourable, however, although he did succeed in finding a publisher for his only book-length work of fiction, *The Narrative of Arthur Gordon Pym*. He had high hopes of this book earning for him a considerable reputation in Britain and the United States, but, in common with almost all his work published in his lifetime, it did not sell widely.

In the summer of 1838 he moved to Philadelphia where, after a year of precarious freelance journalism, he obtained a position as assistant editor of *Burton's Gentleman's Magazine*. This marked the beginning of the happiest and most creative period in his adult life. Not only were these Philadelphia years (1838–44) the years in which Poe demonstrated conclusively his abilities as an editor – first on the staff of *Burton's* and then as editor of *Graham's Magazine* – but it was a period of intensive literary activity during which he composed much of his very finest work. To these years belong such stories as 'The Fall of the House of Usher', 'William Wilson', 'The Murders in the Rue Morgue' and 'The Gold-Bug'. A collection of his short stories, under the title *Tales of the Grotesque and Arabesque*, was published in two volumes in 1840 (the only payment he received for this was twenty free copies for distribution to friends). From this point onwards Poe's life was dominated by two overriding aims – an ambition to make a permanent mark as a man of letters, and to become editor and proprietor of a literary journal which would set the highest possible critical standards. He spent the remainder of his short life in active pursuit of this twin objective.

In January 1842 Virginia ruptured a blood vessel while singing. This was the onset of a steady deterioration in her health which caused him years of anguish. Despite the torment her illness must have meant to him, he worked on, producing the tales which have since earned for him a world-wide reputation: 'The Pit and the Pendulum', 'The Tell-Tale Heart', 'The Black Cat', and many others. He also spent much time and effort trying to raise funds for a periodical of his own, but in this he was unsuccessful.

In April 1844 he returned to New York, which was to remain his home until his death. The sensation produced by the publication of his poem 'The Raven' in January of the following year made his name renowned for the first time throughout the United States. On the strength of this he obtained for a short period a minor position on the New York *Evening Mirror*, whose editor, N. P. Willis, described Poe as 'a quiet, patient, industrious, and most gentlemanly person, commanding the utmost respect and good feeling by his unvarying deportment and ability'. Two further collections of his work, *Tales* (a compilation of twelve short stories) and *The Raven and Other Poems* (a collection of thirty of his best poems) were published in that year by Wiley and Putnam of New York and London, but again on conditions highly unfavourable to the author. For the *Tales* he had submitted seventy stories and articles to the publisher, hoping that the volume would demonstrate the versatility of his talent. Only twelve were selected, however; the book sold for fifty cents a copy, of which Poe received a royalty of eight cents. For *The Raven* he received no royalty but only a lump sum payment of seventy-five dollars.

Throughout most of 1845 he worked on the *Broadway Journal*, a newly founded paper on which for a time he pinned his hopes of establishing a vehicle for his talents. He became in turn editor and sole proprietor, but he was fighting a losing battle against financial difficulties and in January 1846 the magazine ceased publication. Some months later he moved with his family to a cottage at Fordham, then a country district thirteen miles from New York. His wife was clearly very ill and, after a winter of wretched poverty, she died in January 1847 aged twenty-four. Beside himself with grief, he plunged into the writing of 'Eureka', a long prose-poem in which he set out in mystical form his theories of the universe. In this last period of his life he wrote some of his finest poems, including 'Ulalume' and 'The Bells', and two of his most deeply felt short stories, 'The Cask of Amontillado' and 'Hop-Frog'. His own health was now visibly deteriorating. Sensing perhaps that his ambitions were slipping from his grasp, he began to crave feminine sympathy and understanding. He paid court to a number of women of his acquaintance, including Mrs. Sarah Helen Whitman, Mrs. Nancy Richmond ('Annie'), and Sarah Elmira Royster, whom he had loved as a youth and who was now a well-to-do widow. More than one of these ladies reciprocated his attentions, but none of the friendships ended in marriage, although Sarah Royster did consent to become engaged to him. Poe was by this time an unstable figure increasingly seeking refuge from his worries in alcohol and hallucinations.

To the end he cherished his ambition to own his own magazine, and in the summer of 1849 he embarked on a journey to try to raise funds for this project, visiting Richmond, Norfolk and Philadelphia lecturing on 'The Poetic Principle'. While en route from Richmond to New York he was found unconscious in Baltimore on 3 October. It was election time in Baltimore and Poe had apparently been drugged (or made drunk) by hoodlums and then used as a repeater in fraudulent voting. The effect of this experience was too much for his weak heart[3] and, after several days of delirium and exhaustion, he died in hospital on 7 October 1849. His last words, according to witnesses, were 'God help my poor soul!' Three days later his old friend John Kennedy wrote of him: 'Poor Poe! He was an original and exquisite poet, and one of the best prose critics in this country. His works are among the very best of their kind.'

*   *   *   *   *

Viewing the forty years of his life in perspective, it is possible to identify the dominant influences which helped to shape the mind, outlook and achievements of Edgar Allan Poe. These are, firstly, the death of his mother and father and the attempts he made throughout his life to fill the vacuum caused by their death; the distinctive influence of his years in England

and of his Scotch-Irish ancestry; and the literary conditions in the America of the early nineteenth century in which he lived and worked.

His mother died before his third birthday. Though it is questionable, therefore, whether he could remember her in any detail it is certain that he cherished a miniature of her for many years and that he retained an idealised impression in his mind of his gentle, talented English mother. All the other women who played an important role in his life – Frances Allan, Jane Stanard, Maria Clemm, Virginia Clemm – were to greater or lesser degree surrogates for this departed figure. That so many of them died prematurely in tragic circumstances strengthened his conviction of the transience of earthly beauty and happiness. All his life was in a sense a quest for permanent security and affection which continually eluded him.

His father died or disappeared when he was still an infant, and again he cannot have remembered him. Yet he clearly felt the need for a father-figure in his life. Writing years later to a relative, he observed: 'Thus we were left orphans at an age when the hand of a parent is so peculiarly requisite.' For many years John Allan filled the role of a father in his life, and despite their totally dissimilar temperaments there were phases of genuine affection when Poe addressed him as 'Dear Pa' and was encouraged to regard him as his own father. It is in any estimation of Poe's life impossible to overestimate the dominating influence of John Allan; their lives were intimately connected for more than thirty years – from Poe's adoption in 1811 to Allan's death in 1834. The relationship between them was a complex one, more complex perhaps than most biographers have acknowledged.[4] That each in his own way loved the other there can be little doubt. There can also be little doubt that the tension between the proud, dour, forceful Scot and his sensitive, imaginative adopted son produced one of the greatest tragedies in the history of our literature. It is idle to speculate on what might have been had Allan been of a different temperament or had encouraged Poe in his literary ambitions. What is certain is that Poe had been brought up in the expectation that he would ultimately inherit some part of Allan's fortune; the severance of that expectation threw him irrevocably on his own resources.

Writing to his cousin William Poe in 1835 he commented: 'Brought up to no profession, and educated in the expectation of an immense fortune . . . the blow has been a heavy one, and I had nearly succumbed to its influence, and yielded to despair.' The influence of England and English culture upon Poe and his writings is a fascinating one. David Sinclair has expressed this influence well in these terms:

> The first-time reader of Edgar Allan Poe's more popular works could perhaps be forgiven for thinking that he was an English writer – his elaborate, even luxuriant style, his backdrops of ruined castles and palaces with their rich but tasteful draperies, his damp and misty landscapes, his obsession with ancestry and tradition – all have the feel, almost the smell of England. Much of this is derivative, borrowed from English and other European authors, but there is no doubting the influence of four and a half boyhood years in England.[5]

As a result of his years of schooling and travelling in England and Scotland Poe had seen, long before most of his American contemporaries, the beginnings of the Industrial Revolution and the dawn of the railway age. He had seen cities such as London, Liverpool and Newcastle and must have been struck by the sharpest contrasts between them and the open landscape he had known in Virginia. Above all he had come into intimate contact with English culture and traditions, heard the language spoken at its source and imbibed the atmosphere of an ancient civilisation. These influences were to have the deepest impression on his poetry and prose. It should be noted in this connection that Poe himself was predominantly of British stock. His ancestry on his father's side was Scotch-Irish; on his mother's side it was English; this pattern remains true for as far back as it can be traced. This has to be taken into account in any assessment of Poe as a man and as a writer, and it inevitably played an important part in moulding his personality and imagination.

Yet it remains true that in the final analysis he can only be fully understood in his context as an American writer. He lived in the age of slavery and violent unrest and his struggle to win recognition as an imaginative writer was conducted against a background of a new nation striving to achieve cultural and economic independence of England. He was a contemporary of Hawthorne, Emerson, Irving and Long-fellow and whilst he was shaped in part by American culture he sought all his life to attain a style and manner of his own. He helped to shape the literature of the newly emerging United States of America, but had to do this in a relatively untried literary climate and at a time when it was extremely difficult for an aspiring author with no national reputation to interest publishers in his work. Summing up his life and achievements, Philip Van Doren Stern has pithily observed:

> He gave us much and received pathetically little in return, for he was all his life a starveling poet and a miserably paid writer for ephemeral magazines. It is a final irony that his letters and manuscripts have become the most valuable of all American writers.[6]

Poe's Literary Reputation

In 1841 Poe met an influential editor named Rufus W. Griswold, a clergyman who had drifted into editorial work in New York. He seems to have been something of a literary charlatan and had acquired a reputation for himself as an editor and author. Poe was unwise enough to appoint Griswold as his literary executor, not realising that Griswold in fact hated him.

Immediately after Poe's death he inserted a highly critical assessment of Poe's life and works in the *New York Daily Tribune* under the pseudonym 'Ludwig'.[1] The article not only contained a number of falsehoods in its account of Poe's background but amounted to an attack on all he had stood for. It fostered the legend of Poe's 'dissipated life' and vilified him as 'a dissector of sentences' and 'little better than a carping grammarian'. Griswold then proceeded to edit Poe's works in four volumes, including a 'Memoir' which was even more critical and unreliable than the 'Ludwig' article. These two articles did untold damage to Poe's reputation in Britain and the United States, for Griswold's interpretation of him was accepted as authoritative. Even though many of those who had known and worked with Poe – including N. P. Willis, Sarah Whitman and George Graham – came vigorously to his defence, Poe's reputation was blackened for many years as a result of Griswold's falsehoods and insinuations.

It was only when Charles Baudelaire in France began to write appreciations of Poe (from 1852–7) and to translate his writings that the critical tide began to turn. As a result of Baudelaire's espousal of Poe, and appreciations by such writers as Walt Whitman and Bernard Shaw, his life and writings began to be re-examined and viewed in a more dispassionate context. It is only in the last forty years, with the aid of carefully researched biographies and scholarly editions of his prose, poetry and letters, that it has been possible to view his life and work in its totality and to attempt an unemotional appraisal of his character and achievement. Today, thanks in part to the availability of his work in a wide variety of popular editions, and in part to numerous film adaptations based on his stories, his name is known throughout Europe and America and his works are being increasingly translated into foreign languages. The fame which constantly eluded him in life has come to him at last a century and a quarter after his death.

* * * * *

Almost a century passed after his death before American critics began to treat his work with the scholarly attention it merited – indeed, it was not until the publication in 1941 of Arthur Hobson Quinn's definitive study *Edgar Allan Poe: A Critical Biography* that some of the misconceptions surrounding Poe were finally dispelled and he began to be viewed as a serious literary artist. European critics were less slow to recognise his importance, possibly because his relationship to the European Romantic tradition of Shelley, Keats and Byron is more readily discernible than to any American tradition. The failure for so long to acknowledge the essential *seriousness* of his work is traceable to a number of factors, not the least of which was the widespread acceptance of the conception of Poe as a dope addict and inveterate drunkard: an idea sedulously fostered by Griswold and other critics. The failure stems partly from the nature of the stories themselves and the lack, until comparatively recent times, of any recognition of their complexity and coherence as works of art.

There has been much criticism of the narrators of such tales as 'The Tell-Tale Heart', 'The Black Cat' and 'Berenice' – the half-crazed, mumbling psychopaths who protest so vehemently their sanity and reason whilst confessing to atrocious acts of violence – and a tendency to identify Poe himself with these creations. In a perceptive essay[2] James Gargano has demonstrated that to confuse the narrator with the author in these instances is a dangerous over-simplification. The reality is more complex: 'Poe's narrators possess a character and consciousness distinct from those of their creator. These protagonists, I am convinced, speak their own thoughts and are the dupes of their own passions . . . Poe, I maintain, is a serious artist who explores the neuroses of his characters with probing intelligence'. It is precisely this failure to distinguish between the author and the ostensible narrator which has led to so much facile criticism of Poe in the past and to his dismissal as a hysterical purveyor of horror stories, a hack writer who indulged for the sake of sensationalism in cheap effects and absurd Gothic trappings. The narrator of 'The Black Cat' is not Poe any more than the narrator of 'The Cask of Amontillado': he is a completely separate, invented personality with his own character, motivations and weaknesses. Poe's craftsmanship as a writer lay not only in his ability to create an atmosphere of terror and suspense – an ability which few of his many imitators have equalled – but in his capacity to invent a wholly imaginary persona, totally alien in many cases to himself.

None of this explains the reasons for his continuing popularity as a short story writer or the secret of his extraordinary mastery of the short story, more especially the narrative of mystery and horror, as an art form. Why is it that his tales have continued to be read and admired and that his popularity shows no sign of abating? What is it which makes 'The Fall of the House of Usher' and 'The Gold-Bug' (for example) such fascinating tales and the reading of them both an emotional and an intellectual experience? Wherein, in short, lies the essence of Poe's appeal? His appeal lies, I suggest, in the timeless quality of the best of his tales and their continuing relevance to the human condition. He returned repeatedly in his writings to the theme of the 'outsider', to the hero as a lonely and withdrawn figure caught up in a web of machinations and torments. Such a theme struck few chords in the mid-nineteenth century but to our own age, familiar as we are with such figures as Joseph K. in Kafka's *The Trial* and Winston Smith in Orwell's *Nineteen Eighty-Four*, the image of the pursued and persecuted hero who is overwhelmed by torments is all too recognisable. The terror awaiting those who step out of society was a theme which fascinated him and which is vividly communicated in such tales as 'The Pit and the Pendulum':

> These shadows of memory tell, indistinctly, of tall figures that lifted and bore me in silence down – down – still down – till a hideous dizziness oppressed me at the mere idea of the interminableness of the descent. They tell also of a vague horror at my heart, on account of that heart's unnatural stillness . . . . After this I call to mind flatness and dampness: and then all is *madness* – the madness of a memory which busies itself among forbidden things.

It is this ability to describe the sensations of the individual driven to the verge of madness, to write with insight and conviction of those who are 'obsessively engaged in exploring the irrational contours of their own minds'[3] which has proved to be Poe's greatest strength and has led to such widespread acclaim for his work in the twentieth century. Sufficient is now known of his life and circumstances to make it evident that he was in his private self – for much of his life at least – a deeply disturbed and divided figure. But to interpret his work from a solely autobiographical standpoint is misleading; to do so is to underestimate the deliberate craftsmanship of his stories and the seriousness of his intentions as an imaginative writer. His skill and artistry as a storyteller will be examined in detail in later sections of this *Companion* – suffice it to note here that he was from the outset of his career consciously striving to achieve technical excellence in all he undertook and that in both poetry and prose he sought to conform to the highest possible critical standards. In his review of Hawthorne's *Twice-Told Tales* (1842) he outlined his theory of the short story as an art form aiming at a single effect:

> In the whole composition there should be no word written of which the tendency, direct or indirect, is not to the one pre-established design. And by such means, with such care and skill, a picture is at length painted which leaves in the mind of him who contemplates it with a kindred art, a sense of the fullest satisfaction.

There had of course been memorable short stories written before Poe's time, but he was the first to develop the short story as a distinctive art form and to elaborate criteria by which it could be judged. The seriousness with which he approached his own work is evident from the meticulous care with which he revised his tales and poems throughout his life. He was an obsessive reviser, reshaping and polishing the best of his writings until he was absolutely satisfied with them as artistic creations.

Much criticism has been levelled against his characters and settings on the grounds of their remoteness from normal life. Many of his characters withdraw from the world of reality into remote valleys ('Eleonora'), decaying cities ('Ligeia') crumbling mansions ('The Fall of the House of Usher') or secluded abbeys ('The Masque of the Red Death') where they lead a life almost totally removed from everyday human experience. There is undoubtedly some substance in this criticism, but to dismiss them on these grounds alone is too simplistic. All of Poe's central characters develop *as a direct outcome of their detachment* an acuteness of vision, an other-worldly perception, which is communicated vividly to the reader and which intensifies the effect he seeks to create. It is precisely Roderick Usher's insanity which makes 'The Fall of the House of Usher' such a memorable story; his heroes are almost always men and women who, through mental illness or opiates or grief, experience a heightening of consciousness, an enlargement of the boundaries of knowledge, which is shared vicariously with the reader. His critics are on firmer ground in protesting against the limited range of his work and his failure to depict recognisable human situations portraying the development of character. In fact the range of his achievement is much wider than is commonly supposed, for it includes, apart from the tales and poems by which he is mainly known, humorous essays, satires, scientific fantasias, philosophical essays, and a substantial body of literary criticism. Yet it remains true that the novel in the conventional sense was quite outside his range and with few exceptions – for example, 'The Gold-Bug' and parts of *The Narrative of Arthur Gordon Pym* – there is little trace in his work of situations depicting normal human relationships and the nuances of conversation and friendship. In part this was deliberate: Poe consciously eschewed the novel as an art form, believing that the short story was the supreme form of literary expression. In part the explanation lies in the circumstances of his life and the conditions in which he wrote: given the hand-to-mouth existence which he was compelled to adopt for much of his working career it is astonishing that he succeeded in writing as much as he did, and so much of a consistently high standard.

Perhaps the most fascinating aspect of Poe's work from the standpoint of the modern reader is the way in which it illuminates man's mental world. His tales are unique because of their obsessive concern with the darker regions of the mind, with their nightmarish journeys into unexplored depths of mental and spiritual experience. Again and again in his narratives there is a descent, actual or symbolic, into a nether world – a pit, a tomb, a vault, a whirlpool – through which the hero attains release from the external world and the loss of the self. The prisoner in 'The Pit and the Pendulum', the voyager in 'MS. Found in a Bottle', the fisherman in 'A Descent into the Maelstrom', the narrator in 'The Fall of the House of Usher' – all experience a descent into a nightmare world which lies so close to human knowledge and yet which few writers have described with such intense conviction. The *vividness* of Poe's impressions lies in his uncanny ability to involve the reader directly in the spiritual and psychological torments of his characters; the reader becomes a participant, sharing with the narrator the trauma of his experience. It is with an effect of recognition that the twentieth-century reader responds to these situations, acknowledging beneath the Gothic encrustations an illumination of the mind. Living in the aftermath of two world wars, in a century which has witnessed violence and torture on an unparalleled scale, we are perhaps better able to respond to his effects than were the readers and critics of his own generation. His ability to describe the depths of mental torment, to descend imaginatively into the maelström of the human mind, to pass beyond the narrow frontier dividing reason from insanity, is one of his greatest gifts and will continue to give his work relevance in the centuries yet to come.

Reflecting on his life and work as a whole, one is principally impressed with the inner strength which enabled him to continue writing in the most unfavourable conditions. Even in circumstances of the most grinding poverty he could still produce work of the calibre of 'The Mystery of Marie Rogêt' and 'The Landscape Garden'; stricken with grief at the death of his wife he could produce such a work of art as 'Eureka'; at the end of his life, tired, disillusioned and ill, he was yet capable of such a carefully-written tale as 'Hop-Frog'. It was this inner strength, this detachment, this fierce determination to be a writer regardless of his personal circumstances which proved to be Poe's greatest asset. Without it he would have achieved little; with its aid he produced a body of work which, though limited in range and uneven in quality, has carried his name and reputation throughout Europe and the English-speaking world.

Writing to a friend in the last year of his life, he stated:

> Literature is the most noble of professions. In fact, it is about the only one fit for a man. For my own part, there is no seducing me from the path. I shall be a litterateur at least, all my life; nor would I abandon the hopes which still lead me on for all the gold in California.[4]

Poe in retrospect seems a curiously isolated figure, his isolation stemming in large measure from his remoteness from the literary fashions and conventions of his time. He seems indeed to belong to a category all of his own rather than to follow in any recognisable tradition of American letters. Though he derives many of his themes and concerns from the European Romantic tradition of Byron and the Shelley circle, and though he was on occasion guilty of plagiarism, the individuality of his voice is unmistakable and there could be no stronger testimony to the continuing relevance of his work than that virtually the whole corpus of his writings – fiction, poetry and essays – have survived intact into our own century when much of the work of his contemporaries is forgotten. Clearly his writings must possess some quality, some distinctive feature, which readers of succeeding generations have found relevant to their own concerns. This quality lies, I have suggested, in his unrivalled ability to enter the dark regions of man's mental world, to explore the hidden depths of the human psyche and expose the fears, uncertainties and ir-rationalities which lie beneath the facade of normal be-haviour. This in itself, however, would not be sufficient to explain the continuing popularity of his works in many different languages and cultures. To identify the enduring elements in Poe it is necessary to examine his writings, and particularly the short stories, more closely.

The essential theme of many of the stories is that of the doomed and isolated figure – the narrator in 'The Black Cat' and 'The Tell-Tale Heart', the murderer in 'The Imp of the Perverse', the prisoner in 'The Pit and the Pendulum', the avenger in 'The Cask of Amontillado' – who undergoes experiences beyond the range of the normal and communicates them to the reader with an intensity which enables us to *participate vicariously* in all he describes. By identifying ourselves with Poe's narrators we experience emotions and sensations beyond the reach of everyday humanity and enter a world much closer to that of the mentally abnormal. Thus, we experience the urge to kill ('The Imp of the Perverse' and 'The Tell-Tale Heart'), to pursue relentlessly ('The Man of the Crowd'), to be incarcerated and tortured ('The Pit and the Pendulum'), to be sucked into a whirl pool ('A Descent into the Maelstrom'), to be buried alive ('The Premature Burial'). It is this characteristic of his stories, their ability to provide an experience beyond the literary, to describe emotional and mental states outside the range of normal feeling, which explains their continuing relevance to our own age.

Poe himself was well aware of the thin dividing line between rational and irrational behaviour. This was a man who sought release from intolerable sorrows in alcohol, whose wife and mother both died prematurely of disease and who at the end of his life, on his fateful trip to Baltimore, imagined himself to be pursued by a gang intent on murdering him. Through his stories the reader identifies himself with his central characters and becomes one with them in experiencing a whole range of human emotions – guilt, terror, claustrophobia, desire, hatred and suffering. So obsessive is his storytelling, his power to create an atmosphere, his gift of conveying to the reader the spectrum of moods and sensations experienced by his narrators, that disbelief is suspended and the reader finds himself being drawn almost against his will into a nightmare world of horror, violence and cruelty. The sensations of a murderer about to despatch his victim, of a husband tormented by the memory of his dead wife, of a hypnotist attempting to awaken a dead man, of a profligate confronted by his accusing 'better self': all these are described with unforgettable vividness.

In his illuminating essay 'Charles Dickens', George Orwell perceptively observed: 'Much that he [Dickens] wrote is extremely factual, and in the power of evoking visual images he has probably never been equalled. When Dickens has once described something you see it for the rest of your life.' One has only to consider this observation in relation to Poe to recognise at once his strengths and weaknesses as a creative artist. One would search his fiction in vain for any character as fully drawn as (for example) Mr. Micawber or Uriah Heep, yet how vivid are his characters and how intensely wrought are his visual impressions. No one who has read 'The Fall of the House of Usher' can ever forget the description of Roderick Usher immersed with his books in the crumbling, gloomy mansion, while a single reading of 'The Gold-Bug' is sufficient to fix indelibly in the memory a picture of the recluse William Legrand sitting by the fire and describing with enthusiasm his discovery of a new species of beetle. The *intensity* of his visual effects is such as to render them ineffaceable. One thinks, for example, of Valdemar awaking from his mesmeric trance, of the dying Madeline Usher collapsing upon the body of her hapless brother, of the entry of the ape into the bedchamber of Madame L'Espanaye, of the climax of the masked ball in 'The Masque of the Red Death', of the nitre-encrusted catacombs in 'The Cask of Amontillado'. Herein lies his peculiar strength: the ability to convey in concise terms an image, or a series of images, with such clarity as to render the impression unforgettable. Beyond this, his strength lay in the description of mental and emotional states, in removing the layers of artifice from man's animal nature and affording a terrifying glimpse into the violence and sadism present beneath. No one has excelled Poe in his capacity to describe elemental passions and fears, to give voice to the nameless terrors and emotions which on occasion afflict us all. It was his misfortune that in his own lifetime these distinctive gifts were not recognised and that his idiosyncratic world-view failed to meet with the response it merited.

* * * * *

It is a remarkable tribute to the enduring quality of Poe's work that, although much of it was written for provincial newspapers and ephemeral magazines, such a substantial body of work has come down to us. Today, such is his renown, it would be difficult to think of any other writer of his generation whose work is so widely read or which commands such widespread respect.

His influence upon nineteenth and twentieth-century literature has been profound, and has made its mark not only in the English-speaking world but in Europe and Latin America. His influence on European, particularly French, literature has been especially notable. The poetry as translated by Mallarmé and the short stories as translated by Baudelaire have earned for him a renown which has extended into Germany, Russia, Italy and Spain. In England and the United States his reputation has probably never been higher, and he is now accepted as a major figure in the mainstream of the English literary tradition.

It is as a practitioner of the short story as a literary form that he made his most significant contribution to our literature. Not only was he a pioneer in a number of distinct genres – the detective story, the short tale of horror and mystery, the science-fiction narrative – but through these and his critical essays he made an important contribution to our theoretical understanding of the short story as a form of artistic expression. It is in this respect – as an exponent of the short story *as a means of achieving a single memorable effect* on the mind of the reader – that his claim to a permanent place in literary history is most secure.

Part II

AN EDGAR ALLAN POE DICTIONARY

1. Manor House School, Stoke Newington. The school, which stood on the corner of Church Street and Edwards Lane, was attended by Poe from 1817 to 1820. A detailed description of the school and the impression it had on him is contained in his story 'William Wilson'.

2. Rear view of Manor House School. Poe recorded in 'William Wilson': 'But the house! – how quaint an old building was this! – to me how veritably a palace of enchantment!' The five years he spent in England made a deep and lasting impact on the young Poe.

3. Mrs. David Poe, the mother of Edgar Allan Poe. From a contemporary miniature.

4.   The house near 84th Street and Broadway, New York City, in which 'The Raven' was completed in 1844.

TAMERLANE

AND

OTHER POEMS.

BY A BOSTONIAN.

Young heads are giddy. and young hearts are warm,
And make mistakes for manhood to reform.—COWPER.

BOSTON:
CALVIN F. S. THOMAS.....PRINTER.

1827.

5. Title page of *Tamerlane and Other Poems,* 1827. This forty-page pamphlet, printed with yellow paper covers, is one of the rarest of all items of Americana. Only four genuine copies of the first edition are known to exist.

6. Virginia Poe, *née* Clemm, was born in August 1822 and died in January 1847. (From a photograph of a watercolour drawing made after her death.)

For Annie.

All that we see or seem
Is but a dream within a dream.
I stand amid the roar
Of a surf-tormented shore,
And I hold within my hand
Grains of the golden sand —
How few! — yet how they creep
Through my fingers to the deep,
While I weep — while I weep!
Oh, God! can I not grasp
Them with a tighter clasp?
Oh, God! can I not save
One from the pitiless wave?
Is all that I see or seem
But a dream within a dream?

Edgar.

Facsimile of Verses by Edgar Allan Poe.

7. Facsimile of verses by Poe. The neat, regular handwriting is entirely characteristic of him.

8. Poe's cottage at Fordham, where he lived during the closing years of his life. The rustic, romantic setting of the cottage was deeply attractive to Poe and is reflected in such stories as 'The Domain of Arnheim' and 'Landor's Cottage'.

9. Poe in the closing years of his life. (Etched by T. Johnson from a daguerrotype.)

·

An Edgar Allan Poe Dictionary

This dictionary is an alphabetically arranged guide to the titles of all the short stories, essays and poems by Poe published in book form. Reviews of books will be found collected together under the heading 'Book Reviews'.

Details of first publication are given where these are known, but it is important to remember that Poe almost invariably revised his work after publication and that the final texts, as we know them today, frequently differ substantially from the earliest printed versions.

The following abbreviations are used throughout the dictionary:

American	*American Whig Review*
Arthur	*Arthur's Lady's Magazine*
Baltimore	*Baltimore Saturday Visiter*
Bittner	Bittner, William: *Poe, A Biography*
Book	*Baltimore Book*
Broadway	*Broadway Journal*
Burton	*Burton's Gentleman's Magazine*
Chronicle	*Philadelphia Saturday Chronicle*
Columbian	*Columbian Lady's and Gentleman's Magazine*
Companion	*Ladies Companion*
Courier	*Philadelphia Saturday Courier*
Democratic	*United States Magazine and Democratic Review*
Dollar	*The Philadelphia Dollar Newspaper*
Flag	*Flag of Our Union*
Gift	*The Gift*
Godey	*Godey's Lady's Book*

Graham	*Graham's Magazine*
Haining	Haining, Peter: *The Edgar Allan Poe Scrapbook*
Journal	*Home Journal*
Mirror	*New York Evening Mirror*
Monthly	*American Monthly Magazine*
Museum	*Baltimore American Museum*
Opal	*The Opal*
Pioneer	*The Boston Pioneer*
Sartain	*Sartain's Union Magazine*
Saturday	*United States Saturday Post*
SLM	*Southern Literary Messenger*
Snowden	*Snowden's Ladies' Companion*
Sun	*New York Sun*
Tribune	*New York Tribune*
Union	*Union Magazine*
Visiter	*Saturday Morning Visiter*

AL AARAAF. Poem [1829]. The title is taken from *The Koran*, and is the name given to the intermediate realm between heaven and hell. The poem is a discussion on the nature and divinity of beauty.

AL AARAAF, TAMERLANE AND MINOR POEMS. A collection of thirteen poems, including a substantially revised version of 'Tamerlane,' published in *Baltimore* [December 1829].

ALONE. Poem [*circa* 1829] first printed in 1875 from a manuscript apparently in Poe's handwriting. Professor Killis Campbell said of it that 'the case for Poe's authorship, in view of the internal evidence, seems to me to be strong'.

THE AMERICAN DRAMA. Essay [*American*, August 1845] assessing the state of contemporary American drama.

THE ANGEL OF THE ODD. Short story subtitled 'an Extravaganza' [*Columbian*, October 1844]. A humorous account of an encounter with the Angel of the Odd, 'the genius who presided over the contretemps of mankind, and whose business it was to bring about the *odd accidents* which are continually astonishing the sceptic'.

ANNABEL LEE. Poem [*Tribune*, 9 October 1849]. Scholars are generally agreed that the poem refers to Poe's wife, Virginia Clemm, who died at the age of twenty-four. It was published, coincidentally, on the day of Poe's death.

THE ASSIGNATION. Short story [*Godey*, January 1834]. Originally published under the title 'The Visionary'. In Venice the narrator encounters a wealthy Englishman, the lover of an Italian noblewoman. He is invited to the man's residence and there, while admiring his possessions, learns that the noblewoman has been poisoned. He then realises that the Englishman has also been poisoned, apparently by her husband.

AUTOGRAPHY. Essay [*Metropolitan*, September–October 1836] consisting of a critical examination of different styles of handwriting.

THE BALLOON HOAX. Short story [*Sun*, 13 April 1844]. An imaginary and highly circumstantial account of the crossing of the Atlantic by balloon. The story caused a sensation when first published in the *New York Sun* and the offices of the newspaper were besieged by crowds convinced the account was genuine.

A BARGAIN LOST. *See* BON-BON.

THE BELLS. Poem [*Journal*, April 1849], possibly suggested by Marie Louise Shew: Poe's last major poem, notable for onomatopoeia produced by insistent use of repetition.

BERENICE. Short story [*SLM*, March 1835] Berenice and her cousin are brought up together in the same family mansion. The cousin proclaims his love for her but before preparations for their marriage are completed she dies of epilepsy. Her cousin then realises to his horror that she has been buried while still breathing and that, after the interment, he has exhumed the body to extract the teeth which he has long coveted.

THE BLACK CAT. Short story [*Saturday*, 19 August 1843]. The narrator confesses that in a fit of rage he has murdered his wife and walled up her body in the cellar. Whilst police officers are searching the house he realises to his horror that he has buried with her a large cat which he has long detested. The cries of the cat reveal the burial place and lead to the arrest of the murderer.

BON-BON. Short story [*SLM*, December 1835], originally published under the title 'A Bargain Lost'. The tale is a philosophical satire in which a restaurateur encounters the devil; they get drunk together and the devil invites him to sell his soul.

BOOK REVIEWS. Poe wrote a considerable number of book

reviews, of which the following are included in most collected editions of his works:

Anon	*Peter Snook*
Elizabeth Barrett Barrett	*The Drama of Exile*
Robert M. Bird	*The Hawks of Hawk-Hollow*
J. C. C. Brainard	*Poems*
William Cullen Bryant	*Poems*
William Ellery Channing	*Poems*
Henry Cockton	*Stanley Thorn*
J. Fenimore Cooper	*Wyandotté*
Lucretia Davidson	*Poems*
Rufus Dawes	*Poems*
Charles Dickens	*Barnaby Rudge*
	Sketches by Boz
J. Rodman Drake	*The Culprit Fay*
Elizabeth Fries Ellett	*Poems*
Rufus W. Griswold	*The Poets and Poetry of America*
Fitz Greene Halleck	*Alnwick Castle*
William Hazlitt	*The Characters of Shakespeare*
Nathaniel Hawthorne	*Twice-Told Tales*
Joel T. Headley	*The Sacred Mountains*
Henry B. Hirst	*Poems*
R. H. Horne	*Orion: an Epic Poem*
Washington Irving	*Astoria*
Caroline Kirkland	*Poems*
Charles Lever	*Charles O' Malley*
Estelle Anna Lewis	*Poems*
H. W. Longfellow	*Poems*
Augustus Baldwin Longstreet	*Georgia Scenes*
William W. Lord	*Poems*
James Russell Lowell	*A Fable for the Critics*
Thomas Babington Macauley	*Critical and Miscellaneous Essays*
Francis Maryatt	*Joseph Rushbrook*
Cornelius Mathews	*Wakondah*
Margaret Miller	*Poems*
Thomas Moore	*Alciphron*
George P. Morris	*Poems*
William Gilmore Simms	*The Wigwam and the Cabin*

Elizabeth Oakes Smith	*Poems*
Seba Smith	*Powhaton*
J. L. Stephens	*Arabia Petraea*
Bayard Taylor	*Rhymes of Travel*
William Ross Wallace	*Poems*
Robert Walsh	*Didactics*
Thomas Ward	*Poems*
Amelia B. Welby	*Poems*
E. P. Whipple	*Poems*
N. P. Willis	*Tortesa*
L. A. Wilmer	*The Quacks of Helicon*

BRIDAL BALLAD. Poem [January 1837]. The poem may refer to Miss Royster's marriage and her emotions on learning that Poe had not been disloyal as she had been led to believe.

THE BUSINESS MAN. Essay. A satirical attack upon utilitarianism. 'If there is any thing on earth I hate, it is a genius. Your geniuses are all arrant asses – the greater the genius the greater the ass – and to this rule there is no exception whatever.'

THE CASK OF AMONTILLADO. Short story [*Godey*, November 1846]. The narrator describes his hatred for Fortunato and his decision to seek revenge for the latter's insults. He lures Fortunato into the family vaults under the pretence that they are searching for a cask of Amontillado; at the remote end of the crypt he fetters his enemy to the wall and then bricks him up within the vault.

THE CITY IN THE SEA. Poem [1831] originally published under the title 'The Doomed City'; later revised as 'The City of Sin'. The poem is a powerful expression of the symbolism of the vortex, found frequently in the short stories.

THE COLISEUM. Poem [*Visiter*, 26 October 1833]: a meditation on the grandeur of ancient Rome.

THE COLLOQUY OF MONOS AND UNA. Short story [*Graham*, August 1841]. Cast in the form of an imaginary conversation between two spirits, the story concerns their notion of life after death.

THE CONCHOLOGIST'S FIRST BOOK. A school text book on shells published in Philadelphia [1839]. The preface and introduction were written by Poe, but the book itself is largely paraphrased from other reference works.

THE CONQUEROR WORM. Poem [*Graham*, January 1843]: a meditation on the transience of man. It also forms part of the short story 'Ligeia'.

THE CONVERSATION OF EIROS AND CHARMION. Short story [*Burton*, December 1839]. Cast in the form of an imaginary conversation between two spirits, the story relates the approach of a comet to earth and the destruction of all living things by instantaneous combustion.

A DECIDED LOSS. *See* LOSS OF BREATH.

A DESCENT INTO THE MAELSTROM. Short story [*Graham*, May 1841]. A fisherman and his boat are sucked into the Maelstrom whirlpool during a storm. The fisherman escapes by lashing himself to a barrel but his brother, refusing to leave the boat, is drawn into the vortex.

THE DEVIL IN THE BELFRY. Short story [*Chronicle*, May 1839]. A farcical satire on the credulity of the mob, set in the Dutch borough of Vondervotteimittiss.

DIDDLING CONSIDERED AS ONE OF THE EXACT SCIENCES. Humorous essay originally published under the title 'Raising the Wind', [*Courier*, 14 October 1843]. A review of some of the more common, as well as more ingenious, methods of diddling.

DOINGS OF GOTHAM. A collection of commentaries on New York life contributed to *The Columbia Spy*, edited by Thomas O. Mabbott [Pottsville, Pennsylvania, 1929].

THE DOMAIN OF ARNHEIM. Short story, [*Columbian*, March 1847], originally published under the title 'The Landscape Garden'. An account of a man who uses his vast wealth to create a domain in which nature is wholly tamed. 'Not a dead branch – not a withered leaf – not a stray pebble – not a patch of the brown earth was anywhere visible.'

THE DOOMED CITY. *See* THE CITY IN THE SEA.

A DREAM. Poem [1827], originally untitled: a meditation on lost happiness.

DREAM-LAND. Poem [*Graham*, June 1844]. A vivid description of a journey to 'an ultimate dim Thule.... a wild weird clime that lieth, sublime Out of space – out of Time'. The poem should be compared with 'The Raven', 'Eulalie' and 'Ulalume' for its constant use of refrain.

DREAMS. Poem [1827]: a meditation on the happiness and innocence of youth.

A DREAM WITHIN A DREAM. Poem [1827], originally entitled 'Imitation', presumably in acknowledgement of its indebtedness to Byron.

THE DUKE DE L'OMELETTE. Short story [*SLM* 3 March 1832]. A satirical account of a mortal engaged in battle with the devil. The Duke is a caricature of N. P. Willis, one of the leading literary editors of the day.

ELDORADO. Poem [*Flag*, 21 April 1849], possibly the last to be written by Poe and seen by some critics as symbolic of Poe's aspirations and questing nature.

ELEONORA. Short story [*Gift*, 1842]. The narrator and his cousin Eleonora live in the Valley of Many-Coloured Grass. After an idyllic romance Eleonora dies and the narrator, unable to live with his memories, leaves the valley. In a strange city he meets and falls in love with a beautiful maiden and, finding happiness in wedlock, he is absolved from his vows to his dead cousin.

THE ELK. Short story [*Opal*, 1844] originally published under the title 'Morning on the Wissahiccon'. The narrator describes a visit to a stream near Philadelphia and the great natural beauty of the area. Musing, he sees a magnificent elk and imagines this is a hallucination borne of his reverie about the pre-industrial past. He realises to his chagrin that the elk is not a daydream but is the domestic pet of an English family staying in the district.

AN ENIGMA. Poem [*Sartain*, March 1848]. The name Sarah Anna Lewis is concealed within the poem, and can be read by combining the first letter of the first line with the second letter of the second line, and so on. Cf. 'A Valentine'.

EULALIE – A SONG. Poem [*American*, July 1845]. A hymn of praise to 'the fair and gentle Eulalie' and one of Poe's happiest creations.

EUREKA : A PROSE POEM. A philosophical treatise published in New York [March 1848]. Poe, who evidently regarded 'Eureka' as the culmination of his life's work, stated in the preface that 'it is as a Poem only that I wish it to be judged after I am dead'.

EVENING STAR. Poem [1827]: a short song of praise to the Evening Star, contrasting the glory of its beam with the cold light of the summer moon.

THE FACTS IN THE CASE OF M. VALDEMAR. Short story

[*American*, December 1845]. A man is mesmerised while in the final stages of a fatal illness. He falls into a mesmeric trance, occupying some seven months; an attempt is then made to awaken him, whereupon his body disintegrates. (In England the story was published as a separate pamphlet under the title 'Mesmerism in Articulo Mortis: An Astounding and Horrifying Narrative.')

FAIRY-LAND. Poem [*Yankee*, September 1829]: a dream-like description of a fairy landscape, much influenced by Shelley and Thomas Moore.

THE FALL OF THE HOUSE OF USHER. Short story [*Burton*, September 1839]. A boyhood friend of Roderick Usher proposes to spend some weeks staying with his ill friend. During his stay Roderick's sister dies and is entombed in the family mansion. Later it is discovered that she is still alive; she breaks out of her coffin and, clasping her brother in her death agonies, brings about his own demise.

A FEW WORDS ON SECRET WRITING. Essay [*Graham*, July 1841]. A discussion on the art of devising and solving cryptograms, anticipating some of the techniques employed in 'The Gold-Bug'.

FOR ANNIE. Poem [*Flag*, 28 April 1849]. The 'Annie' of the title is Mrs. Annie Richmond, a close friend of Poe's for many years.

FOUR BEASTS IN ONE. Short story, subtitled 'The Homo-Camelopard' [*SLM*, March 1836]. A satirical fantasy set in Antioch in the year 3830. A King, dressed as a 'camelopard', demands the worship of the people; he is acclaimed by the populace despite his performance of acts of barbarism. The story is a parable on the theme of the unthinking cruelty of men by comparison with the dignity of animals.

THE GOLD-BUG. Short story [*Dollar*, June 1843]. The narrator relates how a close friend, William Legrand, unearths the treasure buried by the pirate Captain Kidd. The story, one of Poe's most celebrated tales, is notable for its ingenious solution of a cryptogram.

THE HAPPIEST DAY, THE HAPPIEST HOUR. Poem [1827], originally untitled: a lament for past happinesses which can never be regained.

THE HAUNTED PALACE. Poem [*Museum*, April 1839]. In a letter to Griswold Poe stated 'By "The Haunted Palace" I meant to imply a mind haunted by Phantoms – a disordered brain.' In addition to being published separately as a poem it also forms part of the short story 'The Fall of the House of Usher'.

HOP-FROG (or, THE EIGHT CHAINED ORANG-OUTANGS). Short story [*Flag*, 17 March 1849]. A court jester, Hop-Frog, incensed at the behaviour of the king towards himself and the girl he loves, persuades the king and his seven friends to dress up as orang-outangs. He then wreaks vengeance upon them by setting them alight.

HOW TO WRITE A BLACKWOOD ARTICLE. Short story [*Museum*, November 1838]. Light-hearted advice on how to write an article for *Blackwood's Magazine*, a journal Poe greatly admired and which was much given to printing ghost stories and accounts of improbable predicaments. Cf. 'A Predicament'.

HYMN. Poem [1835]; arguably Poe's most overtly religious poetry.

IMITATION. *See* A DREAM WITHIN A DREAM.

THE IMP OF THE PERVERSE. Short story [*Graham*, July 1845]. The narrator, an acknowledged victim of perversity, commits the perfect murder by poisoning a candle used by his victim whilst reading in bed. He subsequently inherits his victim's estate and the crime remains undetected until, unable to contain the secret any longer, he confesses after being pursued by a crowd.

THE ISLAND OF THE FAY. Short story [*Graham*, June 1841]. The narrator describes a visit to a remote rivulet and island, which he imagines to be inhabited by fairies. He observes one fairy in particular and speculates on 'the cycle of the brief year of her life'. While he watches the fairy approaches nearer and nearer to her death until at last 'darkness fell over all things, and I beheld her magical figure no more'.

ISRAFEL. Poem [1831]: through the figure of the angel Israfel, symbolic of poetic inspiration, Poe rehearses some of his own theories of the nature of poetry.

THE JOURNAL OF JULIUS RODMAN. A serial story [*Burton*, January–June 1840] purporting to be an account of the 'First Passage across the Rocky Mountains of North America ever achieved by Civilised Man'. The story, which draws upon Washington Irving's *Astoria*, describes the adventures of a traveller on a trapping expedition up the Missouri at the end of the 18th century.

KING PEST. Short story [*SLM*, September 1835]. Set in fourteenth-century London at a time when bubonic plague was rampant, the story describes how two drunken seamen enter by accident 'the stronghold of the pestilence', and in a decaying building, the shop of an undertaker, encounter a bizarre company including the self-styled 'King Pest the First'.

THE LAKE: TO———. Poem [1827]: a sombre reverie on the theme of contemplated suicide.

LANDOR'S COTTAGE. Short story [*Flag*, 9 June 1849], subtitled 'A Pendant to The Domain of Arnheim'. The narrator happens upon 'a fairy-like avenue' in which every aspect of the scenery has been artificially created.

THE LANDSCAPE GARDEN. *See* THE DOMAIN OF ARNHEIM.

LENORE. Poem [1831] originally entitled 'The Paean' and probably suggested by Burger's ballad *Lenore* which was widely popular in England during Poe's lifetime.

LETTER TO B———. Essay, first published under the title 'Letter to Mr.———' as a preface to the *Poems* of 1831, and revised before publication in *SLM* [July 1836]. The 'B———' of the title may refer to Elam Bliss, the publisher of Poe's first volume of poetry.

LIFE IN DEATH. *See* THE OVAL PORTRAIT

LIGEIA. Short story [*Museum*, 18 September 1838]. The husband of Ligeia relates the story of his love for her and of their marriage. Following her death he marries again; his second wife, Rowena, also falls ill and apparently dies. After a series of revivifications he discovers, whilst under the influence of opium, that the body is not that of Rowena but of the lady Ligeia.

THE LIGHTHOUSE. The last short story written by Poe, left unfinished and found among his papers after his death. The story, reminiscent of 'MS. Found in a Bottle', describes the reflections of a man living alone on a lighthouse and the gradual onset of feelings of doubt concerning his safety. [*Notes and Queries*, 25 April 1942 and also reprinted in *Haining*.]

LINES WRITTEN IN AN ALBUM. *See* TO F———S S. O———D.

LIONISING. Short story [*SLM*, May 1835]. The narrator, who

has a splendidly developed nose, shoots an opponent's nose off in a duel. He is then told by his father that it is his opponent who is the real hero: 'the greatness of a lion is in proportion to the size of his proboscis, but .... there is no competing with a lion who has no proboscis at all'.

THE LITERARY LIFE OF THINGUM BOB, ESQUIRE. Short story [*SLM*, December 1844]. A satirical attack on literary charlatans: an aspiring writer copies out passages from Dante, Shakespeare and Homer and submits them to various magazines under a pseudonym; all are rejected as being devoid of literary merit.

THE LITERATI. A series of profiles of 'The Literati of New York', published in *Godey* in six instalments during the summer of 1846 and published in book form (posthumously) in 1850.

LOSS OF BREATH. Short story, originally entitled 'A Decided Loss' and subtitled 'A Tale neither in nor out of *Blackwood*' [*Courier*, 10 November 1832]. During an argument with his wife the narrator discovers that he has completely lost his voice. He sets out on a journey by mail coach but, due to his apparent inability to speak or breathe, he is assumed to be dead. Mistaken for a mail robber, he is hanged and interred in a public vault. He then succeeds in regaining his breath and effects his escape.

MAELZEL'S CHESS PLAYER. Essay [*SLM*, April 1836]. Poe demonstrates, by a process of ratiocination, that the chess player exhibited in the United States by Mr. Maelzel was not operated by an automaton but by a concealed human being.

THE MAN OF THE CROWD. Short story [*Burton*, December 1840]. While sitting at the window of a coffee house in London the narrator amuses himself by observing the behaviour of passers-by. His curiosity is aroused by one person in particular, an old man, and he decides to follow him. He follows the man for a considerable distance but eventually wearies of the jostling crowds and abandons his pursuit, realising that the man refuses to be alone.

THE MAN THAT WAS USED UP. Short story [*Burton*, August 1839]. A satirical account of a Military celebrity, 'hero of the Bugaboo and Kickapoo campaign'. The General is called upon whilst dressing; during the interview it becomes evident that he has an artificial leg, arm, teeth and hair, and that even his voice is enhanced by a machine. He is, in fact, almost wholly artificial – 'the man that was used up'.

MS. FOUND IN A BOTTLE. Short story [*Baltimore*, 19 October 1833]. A wealthy traveller sails from the port of Batavia on a voyage to the Sunda islands but is blown off course by a violent storm. At the height of the storm he leaps on board another ship, 'Discovery', but this is borne down an immense whirlpool on the site of the South Pole. (At the time when Poe was writing it was believed that the Poles were gigantic holes in the surface of the earth.)

MARGINALIA. A series of short essays which Poe contributed to *SLM* and other journals over a period of five years, many apparently gleaned from his commonplace book. The essays, 226 in all, include book reviews, philosophical commentary and aphorisms.

THE MASQUE OF THE RED DEATH. Short story, originally entitled 'The Mask of the Red Death: A Fantasy' [*Graham*, May 1842]. A plague known as the 'red death' devastates the countryside. A prince seeking to escape the plague, retires with his friends to a secluded abbey. The pestilence enters the abbey in the form of a figure dressed to resemble a corpse.

MELLONTA TAUTA. Short story [*Godey*, February 1849]. A satirical account (dated 1 April, 2848) of a voyage by balloon across nineteenth-century America. The title, literally translated, means 'these things are in the future'. Cf. the epigraph to 'The Colloquy of Monos and Una'.

MESMERIC REVELATION. Short story [*Columbian*, August 1844]. An imaginary account of a dialogue with a mesmerised invalid: a theme Poe was to elaborate in 'The Facts in the Case of M. Valdemar'.

METZENGERSTEIN. Short story, subtitled 'In Imitation of the German' [*Courier*, 14 January 1832]. A Hungarian nobleman is possessed by the spirit of an enormous horse which he has first seen depicted on a tapestry. Whilst out riding, his palace is consumed by fire. On his return horse and rider plunge headlong into the flames; the fire immediately dies away and a cloud of smoke in the shape of a charger settles over the battlements.

MORNING ON THE WISSAHICCON. *See* THE ELK.

MORELLA. Short story [*SLM*, April 1835]. Morella, a melancholy and learned woman, dies while giving birth to a daughter. The daughter grows up into the image of her mother and, in time, she too dies. Her father places her body in Morella's tomb but finds no trace of Morella.

THE MURDERS IN THE RUE MORGUE. Short story [*Graham*, April 1841]. Two women are horribly murdered in a house in Paris, apparently without motive. The crime presents the police with a superficially insoluble mystery, but through a process of deduction Dupin arrives at the solution: that the murders have been committed by an orang-outang.

THE MYSTERY OF MARIE ROGÊT. Short story [*Snowden*, November–December 1842, February 1843]. A detailed account of the murder of a Parisian *grisette* which is solved by C. Auguste Dupin. The story is based upon a real murder, that of Mary Cecilia Rogers, which occurred in New York in 1842.

MYSTIFICATION. Short story, originally entitled 'Von Jung'. [*Monthly*, June 1837]. A Hungarian nobleman is challenged to a duel but avoids a confrontation by referring his opponent to an obscure passage in a classic treatise on duelling. The work has all the appearance of profundity but is, in fact, meaningless; the nobleman knows that his antagonist will never admit his inability to understand it.

THE NARRATIVE OF ARTHUR GORDON PYM. Novel [New York: Harper & Brothers, July 1838] originally published (incomplete) in instalments in *SLM*, 1837. Poe's only full-length prose composition, the novel is a graphic account of mutiny and shipwreck on the high seas, culminating in an imaginary journey to the South Pole.

NEVER BET THE DEVIL YOUR HEAD. Short story [*Graham*, September 1841] subtitled 'A Tale with a Moral'. The narrator laments a deceased friend whose method of emphasis was to say 'I'll bet you my head.' He uses the phrase once too often: the devil takes him up on it and wins.

NOTES UPON ENGLISH VERSE. Essay [*Pioneer*, March 1843], the original version of 'The Rationale of Verse'.

THE OBLONG BOX. Short story [*Godey*, September 1844]. The wife of a young artist dies as they are about to embark on a sea voyage. The husband decides to take the body to his wife's mother and arranges to have the embalmed corpse transported on the ship in the guise of a box of merchandise. When it becomes necessary to abandon the ship in a violent storm, the husband refuses to leave the box containing his wife and, tying himself to it, abandons himself to the sea.

THE OVAL PORTRAIT. Short story, originally published under the title 'Life in Death' [*Graham*, April 1842]. While staying at a chateau in the Appenines, a visitor is fascinated by a lifelike portrait of a young girl. He learns that the portrait was painted by the girl's husband and that the girl had died at the moment of completion.

THE PAEAN. *See* LENORE.

THE PHILOSOPHY OF COMPOSITION. Essay [*Graham*, April 1846], ostensibly an analysis of the techniques employed by Poe in writing 'The Raven'. The essay was originally written as a public lecture.

PHILOSOPHY OF FURNITURE. Essay [*Burton*, May, 1840]. A light-hearted survey in which attitudes towards furniture in England and Europe are compared with those in America.

THE PIT AND THE PENDULUM. Short story [*The Gift*, 1843]. A victim of the Spanish Inquisition describes the tortures to which he is subject in a dungeon at Toledo. First he is bound to a framework whilst a huge sickle slowly descends upon him. He succeeds in freeing himself from his bonds only to be forced towards a rat-infested pit by the contraction of the heated walls of the cell.

POEMS. A collection of nine poems published in New York by Elam Bliss [March 1831]. Poe raised subscriptions for the volume prior to his dismissal from West Point.

THE POETIC PRINCIPLE. Essay [*Home Journal*, 31 August 1850], delivered many times as a lecture during the final years of Poe's life. *The Poetic Principle* is the poet's definitive statement of his theory of verse.

THE POWER OF WORDS. Essay [*Democratic*, June 1845]. A conversation between Agathos and Oinos concerning the effect of motion upon the universe. Cf. 'The Colloquy of Monos and Una' and The Conversation of Eiros and Charmion'.

A PREDICAMENT. Short story, subtitled 'The Scythe of Time'. [*Museum*, November 1838]. Poe's conception of a contribution suitable for publication in *Blackwood's* (Cf. 'How to Write a Blackwood Article'.) The narrator, whilst examining the clock tower of a church in Edinburgh, is decapitated by the minute hand.

THE PREMATURE BURIAL. Short story [*Dollar*, 31 July 1844]. An account of a number of instances, some taken from real life and others from dreams, in which persons have been buried alive.

THE PROSE ROMANCES OF EDGAR A. POE. A booklet containing 'The Murders in the Rue Morgue' and 'The Man that was Used Up' published in Philadelphia [Autumn, 1843]. The booklet was intended to be the first of a series, but the project was discontinued – probably through lack of sales.

THE PURLOINED LETTER. Short story [*Gift*, 1845]. A letter containing valuable information is stolen by a state official. The utmost efforts of the police to recover the letter prove fruitless, but Dupin locates it by acting on the assumption that the thief would secrete it in an apparently innocuous place. The story anticipates some of the deductive methods employed by Sir Arthur Conan Doyle in the Sherlock Holmes stories.

RAISING THE WIND. *See* DIDDLING.

THE RATIONALE OF VERSE. Essay [*Graham*, March 1843], in which Poe expounds his philosophy of poetry.

THE RAVEN. Poem [*Mirror*, 29 January 1845]. One of Poe's most celebrated poems, and possibly the work for which he is most renowned in the English-speaking world.

THE RAVEN AND OTHER POEMS. A collection of thirty poems published in New York [November 1845]. The book is dedicated to 'Miss Elizabeth Barrett Barrett, of England .... with the most enthusiastic admiration and with the most sincere esteem'.

RISE INFERNAL SPIRITS. Poem, written at the age of thirteen [1822], and discovered among the files of Ellis & Allan. Reprinted in *Haining*.

ROMANCE. Poem [1829], first published as the Preface to *Tamerlane and Other Poems* and, in an expanded form, as the Introduction to *Poems* (1831).

SCENES FROM 'POLITIAN'. Poem [*SLM*, December 1835]. The plot of 'Politian' is based on a sensational murder committed in Kentucky in 1825, and the subsequent trial, conviction and attempted suicide of the assassin.

SHADOW – A PARABLE. Short story [*SLM*, September 1835]: a

prose poem on the theme of *The Masque of the Red Death* (q.v.) the story describes the futile attempt of a group of people to isolate themselves from a cholera epidemic.

SILENCE – A FABLE. Short story, originally entitled 'Siope' [*Book*, 1838]: a brief prose poem describing an encounter between a demon and a deity in a desolate region of Libya.

SIOPE. *See* SILENCE – A FABLE.

THE SLEEPER. Poem [1831]: a meditation on one of Poe's favourite themes, that of the beautiful female corpse. Cf. the short stories 'Berenice', 'Morella', and 'Ligeia'.

SOME SECRETS OF THE MAGAZINE PRISON-HOUSE. Essay [*Broadway*, 15 February 1845]: a criticism of the conditions under which freelance journalists in Poe's time had to work.

SOME WORDS WITH A MUMMY. Short story [*American*, April 1845]: a revived ancient Egyptian criticises modern society and the irresponsible statements of politicians.

SONNET – SILENCE. Poem [*Burton*, April 1840]: a reflection on the theme of 'the corporate Silence', i.e., physical death as perceivable by the senses.

SONNET – TO SCIENCE. Poem [1829]. Poe stated that the sonnet was intended as a criticism of the 'subtleties which would make poetry a study – not a passion'.

SONNET – TO ZANTE. Poem [*SLM*, January 1837]: an elegiac meditation on the theme of the association of memories with particular locations.

THE SPECTACLES. Short story [*Dollar*, 27 March 1844]. A near-sighted young man is deceived into marrying his own great-great-grandmother: the object of the deception is to teach him not to be so vain as to do without spectacles when he really needed them.

THE SPHINX. Short story [*Arthur*, January 1846]. While looking through an open window the narrator imagines he sees a gigantic insect on a distant hill. He describes the apparition in some detail to his friend, only to learn that the creature, whilst undoubtedly real, is in fact minute in size.

SPIRITS OF THE DEAD. Poem [1827] originally entitled 'Visit of the Dead', apparently inspired by resentment against Sarah Elmira Royster, who broke off her romantic friendship with Poe.

STANZAS. Poem [1827], originally untitled. The verses refer to an experience akin to that described by Wordsworth in

'Intimations of Immortality' – that of a mystical communion with nature leading to a mood of exaltation and momentary detachment from the realities of the everyday world. (Cf. Wells, *The Bulpington of Blup*, pp. 77–80).

THE SYSTEM OF DOCTOR TARR AND PROFESSOR FETHER. Short story [*Graham*, November 1845]. A satirical description of a private lunatic asylum in the South of France, in which the regime is one of extreme leniency. The superintendent himself becomes insane and is admitted as a patient; the keepers are then overpowered, tarred and feathered.

A TALE OF JERUSALEM. Humorous essay [*Courier*, 9 June 1832] set in Jerusalem in the year 3941, in which Poe lampoons the kind of story then currently popular with the readers of *Blackwood's*.

A TALE OF THE RAGGED MOUNTAINS. Short story [*Godey*, April 1844]. A young man, while wandering amidst the mountains near his home, dreams that he is taking part in a series of events occurring in the Indian city of Benares in the year 1780. (Cf. H. G. Wells's short story on a similar theme, 'The Remarkable Case of Davidson's Eyes'.)

TALES BY EDGAR A. POE. A collection of twelve short stories published in New York [June 1845]. The selection was made by Evert A. Duychink, an editor connected with the publishers, Wiley & Putnam, from 70 stories submitted by the author. The stories are:

The Gold-Bug
The Black Cat
Mesmeric Revelation
Lionising
The Fall of the House of Usher
A Descent into the Maelström
The Colloquy of Monos and Una
The Conversation of Eiros and Charmion
The Murders in the Rue Morgue
The Mystery of Marie Rogêt
The Purloined Letter
The Man of the Crowd

TALES OF THE FOLIO CLUB. A series of satirical short stories submitted by Poe to the *Courier* in 1831. Scholars are agreed that the *Tales* included 'Metzengerstein', 'The Duke de l'Omelette', 'A Tale of Jerusalem', 'Loss of Breath', 'Bon-Bon', 'Silence: A Fable', 'MS. Found in a Bottle', and 'Lionising'. (Cf. Bittner, 288–92).

TALES OF THE GROTESQUE AND ARABESQUE. A collection of 24 short stories published (in two volumes) in Philadelphia [December 1839]. Poe stated in the preface that he had written the stories with a view to publication in collected form 'to preserve, as far as a certain point, a certain unity of design'.

TAMERLANE. Poem [1827]: a romantic meditation on the theme of the lost paradise; the hero substitutes ambition for love but his worldly achievement becomes ashes when he finds his Eden is now a lifeless world.

TAMERLANE AND OTHER POEMS, BY A BOSTONIAN. A collection of Poe's early poems, privately printed (by Calvin F. S. Thomas) in Boston [May 1827]. The collection contains 'Tamerlane', 'To ———', 'Dreams', 'Visit of the Dead', 'Evening Star', 'Imitation' (later known as 'A Dream within a Dream'), 'Stanzas', 'A Dream', 'The Happiest Day – The Happiest Hour', 'The Lake'.

THE TELL-TALE HEART. Short story [*Pioneer*, January 1843]. The narrator describes how he came to murder an old man. The body is dismembered and placed beneath the floorboards of the murdered man's chamber. Whilst police officers are searching the house the narrator distinctly hears the muffled heartbeat of the old man. The sound becomes intolerably loud until, unable to contain himself, he confesses to the crime.

THOU ART THE MAN. Short story [*Godey*, November 1844]. A wealthy citizen mysteriously disappears and his nephew is accused of murdering him as circumstantial evidence points in his direction. The narrator establishes the identity of the real murderer and arranges for the corpse to be delivered to him inside a box supposedly containing wine. On the lid being opened, the assassin is confronted with the body of his victim which, in the ventriloquial voice of the narrator, says the words "Thou art the man!".

THE THOUSAND AND SECOND TALE OF SCHEHERAZADE. Short story [*Godey*, February 1845]. A facetious account of how Scheherazade describes to her husband, the king, a series of contemporary inventions – including the railway, the telegraph, the calculating machine and the daguerreotype. The king dismisses them all as lies and has her put to death.

THREE SUNDAYS IN A WEEK. Short story. A young man is told by his grand-uncle that he can marry when three Sundays fall together in the same week: he is able to demonstrate that this has occurred by comparing notes with two sea captains who, having crossed the International Date Line in different directions, are respectively in advance of and behind standard time.

TO ――――. Poem [1829]: This short poem (beginning with the lines 'The bowers whereat, in dreams, I see The Wantonest singing birds') apparently refers to Sarah Royster's rejection of Poe in favour of his rival, Mr. Shelton, who – unlike Poe – was a wealthy man.

TO ――――. Poem [1829]: A short (8 lines only) plea to the reader not to sorrow for the poet's fate – he is merely 'a passer-by'.

TO ―――― ――――. Poem [1827]. The poem, commencing with the line 'I saw thee on thy bridal day', apparently refers to the wedding of Sarah Elmira Royster, a woman whom Poe greatly admired but who rejected his offer of marriage.

TO ―――― ―――― ――――. Poem [*Columbian*, March 1848]: a tribute to Marie Louise Shew, a friend of Poe's. Cf. TO M. L. S――――.

TO F――――. Poem [1835]. One of three poems to Frances Sargent Osgood, the other two being 'to F――――s S. O――――d' and 'A Valentine'.

TO F――――s S. O――――D. Poem [1835], originally entitled 'Lines Written in an Album'. One of three poems to Frances Sargent Osgood, the other two being 'To F――――' and 'A Valentine'.

TO HELEN. Poem [1831] apparently suggested by Poe's friend Mrs. Jane Stith Stanard, who befriended Poe when he was a boy.

TO HELEN. Poem [*Union*, November 1848] addressed to Sarah Helen Whitman, a poetess with whom Poe had a romantic friendship. Not to be confused with preceding item.

TO ISADORE. Poem: a feelingly written tribute to Poe's young wife, Virginia Clemm, who died in tragic circumstances in 1847.

TO M. L. S———. Poem [*Journal*, 13 March 1847]; a tribute to Marie Louise Shew, who nursed Poe and his wife during their illness.

TO MY MOTHER. Poem [*Flag*, 7 July 1849] addressed to Poe's mother-in-law, Mrs. Maria Clemm, who looked after him for many years.

TO ONE IN PARADISE. Poem [*Godey*, January 1834]: a lament for a deceased lover. It also forms part of the short story 'The Assignation'.

TO THE RIVER ———. Poem [1829]: a tribute to a river, 'an emblem of the glow of beauty'. Cf. the lyrical description of the River Wissahiccon in the short story 'The Elk'.

ULALUME – A BALLAD. Poem [*American*, December 1847]. The title may be derived from the Latin *Ulalare* (to wail), and the poem is cast in the form of a dialogue between body and soul.

THE UNPARALLELED ADVENTURE OF ONE HANS PFAALL. Short story [*SLM*, June 1835]. The tale purports to be a circumstantial account of a voyage to the moon by balloon, but in the final paragraphs Poe admits it is nothing more than an ingenious hoax.

A VALENTINE. Poem [*Mirror*, February 1846]. The valentine was intended for Frances Sargent Osgood – the name can be read by combining the first letter of the first line with the second letter of the second line, and so on. Cf. 'To F———s. S. O———d' and 'To F———'.

THE VALLEY OF NIS. *See* THE VALLEY OF UNREST.

THE VALLEY OF UNREST. Poem [1831], originally published under the title 'The Valley of Nis': a sombre description of the abode of the dead, where nothing is motionless – 'nothing save the airs that brood over the magic solitude'.

THE VISIONARY. *See* THE ASSIGNATION.

VISIT OF THE DEAD. *See* SPIRITS OF THE DEAD.

VON JUNG. *See* MYSTIFICATION.

VON KEMPELEN AND HIS DISCOVERY. Essay [*Flag*, 14 April 1849]. An imitation of a scientific report on the alleged discovery of a method of turning lead into gold.

WHY THE LITTLE FRENCHMAN WEARS HIS HAND IN A SLING. Short story [*Chronicle*, circa 1839]: a farcical account, written entirely in Irish brogue, of an encounter between an Irish baronet, his heart's desire, and his French rival.

WILLIAM WILSON. Short story [*Burton*, October 1839]. William Wilson, a pupil at a school in England, is tormented by a boy bearing the same name who imitates his behaviour in every way. Years later Wilson is exposed as a cheat by his namesake and kills him.

The story is notable for its reminiscences of life at Stoke Newington, London, where Poe was a schoolboy from 1818–20.

X-ING A PARAGRAB. Short story [*Flag*, 12 May 1849]. A newspaper finds that all the letters 'O' have been stolen from the printing shop and substitutes instead the letter 'X' – with disastrous results. The story caricatures the rivalries which were common between competing newspapers in Poe's time.

Part III

THE SHORT STORIES

The Short Stories

Poe wrote some forty short stories, ranging in theme through horror and mystery to ratiocination and fantasy. He also wrote humorous essays (as, for example, 'Diddling Considered as one of the Exact Sciences') philosophical prose poems (e.g., 'The Colloquy of Monos and Una') and scientific fantasias (e.g. 'Mellonta Tauta'). During his lifetime a handful of his short stories were collected together under the title *Tales of the Grotesque and Arabesque*, but Poe's attempts to secure the publication of his tales in England met with no success, despite the help of Charles Dickens, whom he had met in Philadelphia in March 1842. On 27 November 1842 Dickens wrote to him in these terms:

> I have mentioned it to publishers with whom I have influence, but they have, one and all, declined the venture. The only consolation I can give you is that I do not believe any collection of detached pieces by an unknown writer, even though he were an Englishman, would be at all likely to find a publisher in this metropolis just now.

It was not until long after Poe's death, with the championship of his reputation by such figures as Baudelaire and Mallarmé, that his tales received increasing popular and critical acclaim. Today the collection *Tales of Mystery and Imagination*, which includes all his finest shorter prose, is known and read throughout the world. It is ironic that these short stories, frequently written in difficult circumstances and published in ephemeral newspapers and magazines, and which certainly brought Poe pathetically little financial reward, are now respected, studied and enjoyed wherever English literature is read.

His own approach to the art of the short story is defined with admirable precision in his essay 'The Philosophy of Composition':

> If any literary work is too long to be read at one sitting, we must be content to dispense with the important effect derivable from unity of impression – for, if two sittings be required, the affairs of the world interfere, and everything like totality is at once destroyed . . .. It appears evident, then, that there is a distinct limit, as regards length, to all works of literary art – the limit of a single sitting . . .

Poe was here acknowledging a profound truth, the validity of which anyone who has attempted to write a short story will verify – that it is much more difficult to write a short work of literary merit than to compose a long narrative. That is to say, the *techniques* involved are different and call for creative skills of a high order. Certainly in his own work he remained steadfast to the principle of the 'single sitting'. With the single exception of *The Narrative of Arthur Gordon Pym* all his finest prose work is cast in the form of the short story of six to twenty pages; the longest, 'The Mystery of Marie Rogêt', extending to some 20,000 words. These tales have earned for Poe a posthumous reputation greater than that enjoyed by any other American writer, with the possible exception of Henry James. He is now acknowledged as one of the undisputed masters of the short story and one of the most potent influences on the literature of the uncanny and bizarre.

It will be convenient to divide the discussion which follows into three broad sections: tales of terror, tales of ratiocination, and tales of satire.

TALES OF TERROR

In June 1833 the *Baltimore Saturday Visiter* announced a prose and poetry competition with 'a premium of fifty dollars for the best Tale and twenty-five dollars for the best Poem', to be submitted by 1 October. Poe submitted one poem, 'The Coliseum', and several short stories which he entitled collec-

tively *Tales of the Folio Club*. These included 'Lionising', 'The
Visionary', 'MS. Found in a Bottle' and possibly also 'A Descent
into the Maelström'. The judges for the competition were
three distinguished Baltimore literary figures – J. H. B. Latrobe, Dr. James H. Miller and John P. Kennedy – the latter a
well known novelist. Announcing the results on 12 October,
the judges awarded the short story prize to 'MS. Found in a
Bottle', being greatly impressed by 'the originality of its
conception and its length'. The judges also commended Poe
on all the stories submitted by him:

> There was genius in everything they listened to; no ill-
> placed punctuation, no worn truisms, no strong thought
> elaborated into weakness. Logic and imagination were
> combined in rare consistency . . . . These tales are eminently
> distinguished by a wild, vigorous, and poetical imagination,
> a rich style, a fertile invention, and varied and curious
> learning.

Although Poe did not win the poetry prize (this was won by
John H. Hewitt, editor of the *Visiter*, who had submitted his
entry under a pseudonym) he could be well pleased with the
overall results. The commendation of 'MS. Found in a Bottle'
represents the first serious recognition he had received; it was
in a real sense the beginning of his literary career. Poe was
twenty-four years of age and was in the earliest stages of
recognition as a master of the short story.

'MS. Found in a Bottle' is written in the vivid documentary
style which Poe was soon to make his own, and which other
writers – most notably H. G. Wells – were later to emulate.
The opening sentence at once establishes the narrator as a
man of education and character:

> Of my country and of my family I have little to say. Ill usage
> and length of years have driven me from the one, and
> estranged me from the other. Hereditary wealth afforded
> me an education of no common order, and a contemplative
> turn of mind enabled me to methodise the stores which
> early study very diligently garnered up.

With this sober, matter-of-fact opening Poe proceeds with

considerable skill to arouse the reader's interest by building
up a detailed picture of the narrator's embarkation on a sea
voyage from Java to the Sunda islands. He had read Captain
Adam Seaborn's *Symzonia, A Voyage of Discovery* (1820) and
Jane Porter's romance *Sir Edward Seaward's Narrative of His
Shipwreck* (1831) and had all his life been fascinated by the sea
and by the tales of seafaring men. His intention in this story
may well have been to parody a number of popular romances
of the day, but his technical skill and verisimilitude are such
that the story is still widely read today and acknowledged as a
masterpiece of carefully sustained tension.

An atmosphere of brooding terror is built up as the onset of
the storm gathers momentum:

> My notice was soon afterwards attracted by the dusky-red
> appearance of the moon, and the peculiar character of the
> sea. The latter was undergoing a rapid change, and the
> water seemed more than usually transparent. Although I
> could distinctly see the bottom, yet, heaving the lead, I
> found the ship in fifteen fathoms. The air now became
> intolerably hot, and was loaded with spiral exhalations
> similar to those arising from heated iron. As night came on,
> every breath of wind died away, and a more entire calm it is
> impossible to conceive.

The description of the storm and the ensuing shipwreck is
notable for its convincing accumulation of detail, a device
Defoe had employed with telling effect in *Robinson Crusoe*.
This had been among Poe's favourite boyhood reading and he
now made good use of the seafaring knowledge he had
acquired from his discursive reading, his talks with sailors (it
has been recorded of him that 'Poe, like Stevenson after him,
would sit hour after hour listening to sailors' yarns of the sea'[1])
and from the five week journey across the Atlantic he had
experienced as a boy. The effect of the amassed circumstantial
detail is to dispel the reader's disbelief and to transform an
apparently incredible narrative into an impressive piece of
factual reportage. Poe was well aware of the considerable
contemporary interest in accounts of journeys to unknown
regions and in the idea of polar exploration. All this he
skilfully capitalises upon, anticipating in the final

paragraphs – in which the hero is borne irresistibly into the polar vortex – the climax of *Arthur Gordon Pym*. Indeed the whole of this short story can be regarded as a first sketch of themes he was later to develop on a much fuller canvas in *Pym*. 'MS. Found in a Bottle' can be read as a powerful tale of adventure in the vein of Stevenson or Verne or, on a deeper level, as an allegory rich in symbolical undertones. Some commentators see the tale as a parable on the theme of death and rebirth, others as a complex interplay of images symbolising the journey of the soul from the womb to self-discovery and ultimate extinction.[2] What is certain is that Poe was heavily influenced by *The Rime of the Ancient Mariner* and drew on Coleridge's poem in describing some of his most haunting images – the ghost ship, the frightful journey towards the South Pole, the ancient, decrepit crew of silent figures – and so on. Moreover, whether consciously or unconsciously, he encapsulated a number of ideas which were to become the central *leit-motifs* of his life.

There is first the obsession with the idea of a *doppel-ganger*: the captain of the ghost ship is the narrator's double. 'I have seen the captain face to face . . .. In stature he is nearly my own height; that is, about five feet eight inches.' The silent, inscrutable double who haunts the narrator and becomes ultimately the agent of his destruction was a theme to which he returned in 'William Wilson': suffice it to say here that for Poe this was unquestionably a powerful imaginative symbol which underlay much of his work. Then the whole story is dominated by imagery of the atmosphere and temperature, vividly contrasting the unnatural calm which precedes the storm followed by the plunging of the world into blackness and nightmare. Already Poe was aware of the deep fountains of despair in his own make-up and was prefiguring that interplay between rationality and impending menace which was to become his distinctive contribution to literature. But above all else the story is permeated by the idea of destruction – of the ship in which the narrator embarks, of his companions, and ultimately of himself.

To conceive the horror of my sensations is, I presume, utterly impossible; yet a curiosity to penetrate the mysteries of these awful regions predominates even over my despair, and will reconcile me to the most hideous aspect of death. It is evident that we are hurrying onwards to some exciting knowledge – some never-to-be-imparted secret, whose attainment is destruction.

The concluding paragraphs of the story offer convincing evidence that the narrator, in common with Poe himself, was both repelled and fascinated by the idea of death. As he rushes towards extinction in the whirlpool he is not afraid – indeed he embraces his imminent death with stoicism and curiosity (it is significant that the ship which bears him with irresistible force to his doom bears the name 'Discovery'). In the young author of 'MS. Found in a Bottle' it is possible to detect the tortured ambivalence of the creator of 'Eureka' and 'The Fall of the House of Usher'.

'Morella' was published in the *Southern Literary Messenger* of April 1835 and again in *Burton's Gentleman's Magazine* for November 1839 and formed one of the series Poe entitled *The Tales of the Folio Club*. During this period he became a principal contributor and virtually the editor of the *Magazine*, which had been founded in 1837 by an Englishman, William Evans Burton. Between August and December 1839 Poe contributed, in addition to 'Morella', 'The Man that was Used Up', 'The Fall of the House of Usher', 'William Wilson', and 'The Conversation of Eiros and Charmion'. Hervey Allen observed that 'To come across Poe's work suddenly in *Burton's* is like finding a sonnet by Michelangelo in a bizarre scrapbook.'[3]

In this short tale of six pages the narrator describes his intellectual attraction for his friend Morella. They marry, although there is no passion between them, yet he is fascinated by her presence.

And then, hour after hour, would I linger by her side, and dwell upon the music of her voice – until, at length, its melody was tainted with terror, – and there fell a shadow upon my soul – and I grew pale, and shuddered inwardly at those too unearthly tones. And thus, joy suddenly faded into horror, and the most beautiful became the most hideous, as Hinnon became Ge-Henna.

Morella sickens and dies, bearing on her deathbed a

daughter bearing a striking resemblance to her mother. At the age of ten the daughter is baptised and is also given the name Morella. When she too dies the narrator carries her body to the tomb but 'laughed with a long and bitter laugh as I found no traces of the first, in the charnel where I laid the second – Morella'.

In common with 'Berenice', written at about the same time, 'Morella' betrays Poe's preoccupation with the idea of premature death (in both stories the narrator describes with morbid relish the onset of illness and decay in his bride) but whereas Thomas White, founder of the *Southern Literary Messenger*, had disliked 'Berenice' as being 'by far too horrible' he was pleased with 'Morella'. Indeed it is arguable that 'Morella' represents a considerable advance on the former story in both literary and imaginative terms and moreover that in both stories Poe was giving fictional expression to the fascination he felt for his cousin Virginia and which he had earlier felt for his mother Elizabeth Arnold.

In a perceptive essay[4] Marie Bonaparte has suggested that the story is in essence a reflection of Poe's own emotional conflict at the time of writing, and that the tale is a fantasia on the theme of transference. At the time when 'Morella' was written Virginia was about ten years of age. It is just at this age that the second Morella is baptised with the name of her dead mother, whom she has become more and more to resemble. It is not too fanciful to suggest then that the story is the symbolic representation of an actual event – the elevation of Virginia from a child to the status of a mother-transference figure. Marie Bonaparte goes on to assert that since 'love from infancy, for Poe, had worn death's aspect', he felt compelled to return again and again to the theme of the ideal woman who sickens and dies – a subject which Poe himself termed 'the most poetical topic in the world'.

When viewed in the context of his total literary work it can be seen that 'Morella' is in a sense a preliminary sketch for 'Ligeia', a tale which many critics have regarded as Poe's finest creation. In its economy of narration, its careful pacing of incident and dénouement and its sombre accretion of an atmosphere of controlled suspense, 'Morella' merits a place in the canon as one of his most revealing stories and one bearing many of the hallmarks of the mature Poe.

In September 1838 Poe submitted his short story, 'Ligeia', to a magazine newly founded in Baltimore, *The American Museum of Literature and the Arts*. The magazine had been started by two of his friends, Dr. Nathan C. Brooks and Dr. Joseph E. Snodgrass and the story appeared in the first issue. Poe was depressed by the apparent poor sales of his romance *The Narrative of Arthur Gordon Pym* and had moved from New York to Philadelphia (at that time one of the foremost publishing centres in the United States) to try and establish a footing in literary circles there. The publication of his work in Baltimore at this time must have been warmly welcome to Poe but it brought him little financial reward – he appears to have been paid the sum of ten dollars for 'Ligeia': a story now acknowledged as one of the handful of tales destined to earn for him literary immortality.

The story tells of a narrator who, overcome with grief at the death of his wife Ligeia, marries 'as the successor of the unforgotten Ligeia' an aristocratic lady, Rowena Trevanion. He settles with his new wife in an abbey in a remote part of England but he is haunted by the memory of his dead love.

> My memory flew back, (oh, with what intensity of regret!) to Ligeia, the beloved, the august, the beautiful, the entombed. I revelled in recollections of her purity, of her wisdom, of her lofty, her ethereal nature, of her passionate, her idolatrous love.

As this vision comes increasingly to dominate his thoughts and emotions he realises that he feels for the Lady Rowena nothing but hatred. At last Rowena falls ill and dies but the corpse appears to the narrator (who confesses at several stages in the narrative to be under the influence of opium) to revive at intervals. With mounting horror the repeated awakening of the body is described, as the corpse gradually assumes the character of the beloved Ligeia. The ghastly climax is reached when the body stands before him and the removal of the cerements reveals not Rowena but the living presence of his departed love.

Hervey Allen has argued that 'Ligeia' provides irrefutable evidence of Poe's addiction to opium.[5] Whether it does or not seems to the present writer to be irrelevant to any discussion of

Poe as a literary figure; in any event the evidence that he was a habitual taker of the drug is inconclusive. What is not in dispute is that in this story he was giving fictional expression to his most deeply felt emotional attitudes. It is at one level an unsurpassed study of terror and insanity; it is also, in common with 'Berenice' and 'Morella', a fantasia on the theme of love conquering the grave. On a deeper level it is a fascinating exploration of the quest of the poetical imagination for celestial beauty. Much of Poe's verse is concerned with the transience and elusiveness of earthly beauty; the narrator of 'Ligeia' is obsessed with the idea of Beauty which he embodies in the dream-like description of his first wife. With the death of Ligeia comes the symbolic end of the storyteller's creative powers, the cessation of all his dreams of knowledge and culture. 'Without Ligeia I was but as a child groping be-nighted.' He attempts to regain his lost vision by deliberately subsiding into opium-induced dreams. It is only with the final transformation of the dead Rowena into the beautiful, un-earthly Ligeia that his quest for loveliness is realised and his imaginative powers are regained.

It is significant that Poe himself regarded 'Ligeia' as his finest story for it embodies beneath its Gothic trappings some of his most characteristic preoccupations – the unnamed and tormented narrator, the death of a beloved spouse, the detailed description of fantastic architecture, the morbid concern with the minutiae of rigor mortis and, above all, the quest for an elusive perfection of knowledge and beauty in the form of an ideal woman. Moreover the story is a remarkable example of that controlled excitement, that skill of narration and dénouement, which are now associated ineradicably with his name. It is these qualities which were to come to the foremost in his next tale.

'The Fall of the House of Usher', one of Poe's most celebrated tales, has earned for him a reputation extending far beyond the English speaking world. Successive film adaptations have kept it before the minds of the public to such an extent that the very title is synonymous with unspeakable horrors. Yet on examination it can be seen that the story is written with care and restraint, that it has allegorical under-tones corresponding to some of his innermost longings, and that its imaginative and mythical qualities are such as to place it in the foremost rank of its genre.

The story begins with what must surely be one of the most well known opening paragraphs in all literature:

> During the whole of a dull, dark, and soundless day in the autumn of the year, when the clouds hung oppressively low in the heavens, I had been passing alone, on horseback, through a singularly dreary tract of country; and at length found myself, as the shades of the evening drew on, within view of the melancholy House of Usher. I know not how it was – but with the first glimpse of the building, a sense of insufferable gloom pervaded my spirit. I say insufferable; for the feeling was unrelieved by any of that half-pleasurable, because poetic, sentiment, with which the mind usually receives even the sternest natural images of the desolate or terrible.

The entire narrative, not least these introductory sentences, is an example of Poe's writing at its best. With considerable skill and economy of words he succeeds in building up an atmosphere of impending horror; indeed the story as a whole is an incomparable study in *atmospherics*. Notice particularly how such touches as 'the clouds hung oppressively low in the heavens' and 'as the shades of the evening drew on' contribute to the gradual accumulation of tension: already at the outset of the story the reader has a sense of a palpable, threatening presence which will gradually become more menacing as the narrative proceeds.

The description of the house itself, of the gloomy apartments in which Usher resides, of the strange and morose Roderick Usher and of his dying sister Madeline, is achieved with an expertise and confidence belying Poe's thirty years. The surface narrative is a composite of material used in 'The Assignation', 'The Premature Burial' and 'Ligeia', but what makes the amalgam so memorable is the skill of the storyteller in blending these melodramatic ingredients – a decaying mansion, a morbid recluse, a body buried alive – into a cohesive and intellectually satisfying work of art. It says much for his talents as a writer that from these gothic components, which in lesser hands would have been simply an excuse for a series of clichés, Poe created a tale which has haunted his readers for nearly 150 years.

Roderick Usher, who 'had been one of my boon companions in boyhood', is one of Poe's most memorable creations. In common with Poe himself (and, significantly, the central character in 'The Gold-Bug'[6]) his moods were 'alternately vivacious and sullen'. Reserved, sensitive, courteous and kindly, Usher is indeed a mirror image of Poe or at least a projection, a doppel-ganger, of himself as he imagined himself to be. 'The Fall of the House of Usher' has fascinated critics for many years, not only because of its literary qualities but also for the insight it affords into Poe's deepest creative visions. What perversity, for example, led him to ascribe to Roderick Usher not simply his own traits and enthusiasms (including his love of old and unusual books) but even his physical appearance?

> Yet the character of his face had been at all times remarkable. A cadaverousness of complexion; an eye large, liquid, and luminous beyond comparison; lips somewhat thin and very pallid, but of a surpassingly beautiful curve; a nose of delicate Hebrew model, but with a breadth of nostril unusual in similar formations; a finely moulded chin, speaking, in its want of prominence, of a want of moral energy; hair of a more than web-like softness and tenuity; these features, with an inordinate expansion above the regions of the temple, made up altogether a countenance not easily to be forgotten.

William Bittner describes the story as a 'penetrating piece of self-analysis'[7] and it is not difficult to see why. Not only does Usher embody many of Poe's own characteristics and weaknesses but the tale as a whole is an extremely interesting fantasia on the theme of the exiled hero – the man of culture who, like William Legrand in 'The Gold-Bug', deliberately shuts himself off from civilisation and lives the life of a recluse. Whereas in most of the short stories the narrator and the hero are one and the same, in this instance some instinct told Poe not to cast the tale in this form. Here the story is told by a disinterested and impartial observer, and as a result we see Usher *from the outside*, as a tortured and unbalanced man consumed by irrational and melancholy fears. It is as if Poe, aware of his divided inner nature, is reflecting on his spiritual or dream-self in the form of an elaborate allegory.

Many of Poe's landscapes have a remarkably dream-like quality but none more so than this one. On his first sight of the House of Usher the narrator is struck by the 'wild inconsistency between its still perfect adaptation of parts, and the crumbling condition of the individual stones'. Usher indeed inhabits a ruined palace of art and the reader has the sense that, with his death, the building itself must come to an end. With the collapse of the house into the waters of the tarn (and such is the symmetry of the story that this is not revealed until the very last line) we are aware that this marks the irrevocable end of the House of Usher – both in the sense of the lineage and the building. In his writings Poe returned again and again to the theme of the transience of art, and it is possible to discern in 'Usher' a restatement of this idée fixe. The mansion occupied by Roderick Usher is a crumbling and decayed Domain of Arnheim; it is a symbol of the impermanence of literature and the arts.

Whether the house described so vividly by Poe was based upon an actual location is debatable. The description sounds so much like a chateau in a remote area of France that it is tempting to think that Poe may have travelled to Europe as a young man. It is much more likely, however, to have been based upon one of the crumbling and abandoned mansions which he must have seen in the Carolina woods when stationed at Charleston. What is more pertinent to an understanding of the story is that Poe was unquestionably haunted by a sense of *loss*: an obsessive awareness of the unattainability of enduring beauty. This is evident in a number of his tales and poems including 'The Domain of Arnheim' (also known as 'The Landscape Garden') and 'The Haunted Palace' and it is this which gives so much of his work a surprisingly modern, twentieth-century quality. In our own time the idea of the 'lost domain' – the elusive world which was experienced in childhood or adolescence but is never recaptured – has found expression in such stories as Alain-Fournier's *Le Grand Meaulnes* and John Fowles's *The Magus*,[8] but in the story of Roderick and Madeline Usher Poe added a new dimension of terror to the eternal quest for a lost happiness.

This tale, then, is in a sense a dream of the narrator's: the moment he crosses the causeway and enters Usher's domain he has left the real world behind him and entered the world of the imagination. It is a journey into the narrator's mental world. There is no gainsaying the power of the story or the haunting quality of the doomed brother and sister who act out their 'mad trist', but in the last analysis it remains much more than a mere horror story. With its perfect symmetry of construction, its unrivalled atmospheric overtones and overall sense of brooding decay the tale merits a permanent place in English literature. Philip Van Doren Stern described it as 'surely one of the great short stories of the world'.

In his next tale, 'William Wilson,' Poe drew heavily on reminiscences of his school days in England and Scotland, synthesising his memories in a powerful allegory of his own dual nature which may have been the inspiration for Stevenson's short story 'Markheim'.

For several months in 1815 he was a pupil at the grammar school at Irvine, Scotland, and then from the autumn of 1817 until May 1820 he attended the Manor House School, Stoke Newington (the school stood on the corner of Church Street and what is now Edwards Lane). It is important to bear in mind that Stoke Newington at that time was several miles from urban London and still retained much of the rural, unhurried atmosphere of an old English village. There can be no doubt that the antique atmosphere of the school and the surrounding village made a powerful impact on Poe's imagination. Although he was only eight years of age at the time of entering it he was not too young to be deeply impressed by its historical and cultural associations and it is not too fanciful to see in this ancient setting, with its green lanes and rows of Queen Anne and Georgian houses, the origins of that fascination with time-worn buildings and romantic milieu which were later to become his hallmark.

The school building described by Poe is not the Manor House Academy (which contemporary prints show to have been a plain, rather sombre house) but rather the Elizabethan mansion across the street to which he tethered his romantic daydreams:

My earliest recollections of a school-life, are connected with a large, rambling, Elizabethan house in a misty-looking village of England, where were a vast number of gigantic and gnarled trees, and where all the houses were excessively ancient. In truth, it was a dream-like and spirit-soothing place, that venerable old town. At this moment, in fancy, I feel the refreshing chilliness of its deeply-shadowed avenues, inhale the fragrance of its thousand shrubberies, and thrill anew with undefinable delight, at the deep hollow note of the church-bell, breaking, each hour, with sullen and sudden roar, upon the stillness of the dusky atmosphere in which the fretted Gothic steeple lay imbedded and asleep.

Poe was already adept at creating an atmosphere of suspense, with the minimum use of words and dramatic effects, and his much quoted description of the house and the school-rooms is among his finest pieces of 'Gothic' writing, forming a backcloth to the introduction of the narrator's doppel-ganger William Wilson. The account of his fascination for his namesake and the gradual shift in his emotions from puzzled embarrassment to utter hatred is done with great skill – indeed it is arguable that 'William Wilson' as a whole is as forceful and atmospheric a piece of writing as any in the canon, yet for some reason, possibly because it lacks the melodramatic qualities of 'Usher' and 'The Tell-Tale Heart', it has never attained the popularity of his other work.

With mounting horror the narrator recounts the haunting of his own life by his pervasive namesake – a double who not only enters the academy on the same day and who imitates his every mannerism but who even has the same date of birth. (In the final revision of the story Wilson's date of birth is given as 19 January 1813, but in earlier versions the date corresponded with Poe's own birthdate – 19 January 1809.) Even after he has left school and entered Oxford Wilson is still pursued by his antagonist, who invariably times his appearances at those moments when the narrator is contemplating some act of criminality. The climax occurs during a carnival at Rome when Wilson is planning the seduction of a beautiful young woman, only to be confronted at the crucial moment by his persecutor. He slays his doppel-ganger with a sword, but the most awesome – and prophetic – moment in the story comes when the dying figure speaks with a voice uncannily resembling his own: 'You have conquered, and I yield . . . . In me didst thou exist – and, in my death, see by this image, which is thine own, how utterly thou hast murdered thyself.'

The confusion and posturing of the egocentric narrator tends to mute the very real literary merits of 'William Wilson'. It has a carefully thought out structure which on examination can be seen to be subtle and deliberate. Especially notable is the gradual development of Wilson's moral depravity and the manner in which Poe's conscious artistic purpose is revealed through the slow elaboration of symbolic detail. The narrator in 'William Wilson' and Poe are not one and the same, and herein lies much of the tale's subtlety. In a real sense there were two Poes. One was the literary figure, the conscientious and dedicated editor, the aspiring poet, the critic who insisted upon the highest standards in all forms of the arts and who wished to leave a permanent mark on American letters; the other was an outcast, a man who sought refuge from intolerable pressures in opium and alcohol, a man who could be rendered incapable by a single glass of wine. Poe was fully aware of this dichotomy in his own temperament and 'William Wilson' is a reflection of the lifelong tension between his two selves. From this standpoint it is the most autobiographical of all his stories, not simply in the description of his school days but, more important, in its symbolic undertones. In this account of a man who continually runs away from his conscience and then at last kills him – in doing so realising he has destroyed his better self and cut himself off from union with God and man – Poe wrote one of his most revealing stories.

'The Oval Portrait' (originally entitled 'Life in Death') marks a return to the preoccupation with life after death which is characteristic of such tales as 'Ligeia' and 'The Assignation'. The portrait is that of a young girl who dies as the painting is completed; yet the artist has created such a perfect and life-like work of art that the image on the canvas appears to be imbued with life itself. In executing the portrait the artist has lost his bride, but he has succeeded in creating an impression of her which will defy time; he has captured her in the painting at the very moment of her most perfect beauty.

One of Poe's most carefully written stories, 'The Oval Portrait' is remarkable for its dream-like, romantic setting; 'one of those piles of commingled gloom and grandeur which have so long frowned among the Apennines, not less in fact than in the fancy of Mrs. Radcliffe'. Within its brief compass Poe succeeds in creating a perfectly structured short story which lingers in the mind long after it has been read. Whatever deeper psychological interpretations may be read into it[9] the story stands on its own merits as an excellent example of its genre which eludes all attempts to define its peculiar hypnotic power.

'The Oval Portrait' was closely followed by 'The Masque of the Red Death', a tale written in Poe's most florid manner and yet one in which the baroque style seems perfectly appropriate to its theme. The story – which may have had its origin in the cholera epidemic which struck Baltimore in 1831 – has been described as 'gruesomely autobiographical',[10] and certainly its preoccupation with 'the redness and the horror of blood' must have owed much to his sad personal circumstances at the time of writing. In January 1842 his wife Virginia broke a blood vessel whilst singing; she suffered a haemorrhage which, he must have known, marked the onset of the final and fatal stage of consumption. The illness was to drag on for five years of agonising suspense; since Poe was deeply devoted to his wife he must have experienced during this time the sufferings of the damned. For a while he sought relief from his torment in alcohol, but he was soon hard at work once again writing critical articles and book reviews for *Graham's Magazine*, including one on *Barnaby Rudge* in which he correctly forecast the outcome of Dickens's complicated plot.

'The Masque of the Red Death' was written in the weeks immediately following Virginia's collapse, when he was living in constant expectation of another haemorrhage. It describes a Prince Prospero who, together with a thousand friends, retires to a remote abbey in order to escape a pestilence, the 'Red Death', which has devastated his country. One night during a masquerade a mysterious mummer appears in their midst dressed like a victim of the plague. He is pursued through the seven connected rooms in which the masked ball is held and finally cornered by the Prince himself. On approaching him the Prince falls down dead, whereupon the mummer is seized by a throng of enraged revellers. To their horror the revellers find that, on removing the corpse-like mask from the figure, he is 'untenanted by any tangible form': the cadaverous form is empty. Simultaneously comes the realisation that the figure has brought with it the Red Death; the epidemic spreads with terrifying rapidity through the abbey until at last 'Darkness and Decay and the Red Death held illimitable dominion over all'. With this unforgettably powerful visual image Poe brings to an end one of his most nightmarish and haunting tales.

The dream-like quality of the story, which Poe skilfully achieves with an accumulation of linguistic devices, serves to heighten its allegorical intention – for it has, in my view, a symbolic as well as a literal interpretation. The Red Death may be taken as a symbol for that materialistic rationalism so prevalent in Poe's time – rationalism which in his critical writings he likened to a creeping pestilence. Prince Prospero's attempt to flee from the consequences of the plague and find refuge in the seclusion of the walled abbey signifies the flight of the imagination from consciousness into dream and reverie. (It is significant in this connection that the revellers at the masquerade are described as 'a multitude of dreams', and as 'delirious fancies such as the madman fashions'.) On this interpretation the strange figure disguised as a corpse is symbolic of consciousness and his coming means the end of the masquerade – the ending of dreams. The conclusion of the story is thus both ambivalent and disturbing: the assertion that only through the death of a vital part of oneself can the creative artist free himself from earthly considerations. As a theory of life and art Poe's argument must seem to modern readers negative and incomplete, yet it is fully consistent with all that had gone before.

It should be remarked in passing that the treatment of *time* in the story is extremely interesting. A huge ebony clock which chimes loudly each hour stands against the wall of the end apartment; the revelry momentarily ceases each time the clock strikes. The tall masked figure dressed 'in the habiliments of the grave' appears in the ballroom as the strokes of midnight are heard and, when he is finally seized, he is standing in the shadow of the clock. When the last of the revellers has fallen victim to the disease the clock ceases to tick. This haunting obsession with time, and with the insistent rhythm of the pendulum (so strongly suggestive of the beat of the human heart) was one which Poe introduced to brilliant effect in 'The Pit and the Pendulum' and 'The Tell-Tale Heart'. In 'The Masque' it becomes a powerful motif of the temporality of earthly passions.

This story, then, was written at a time when Poe was in a torment of uncertainty. It says much for his intellectual qualities that he was capable of producing such carefully composed work at such a time of mental anguish. Whether he was influenced by Mary Shelley's novel *The Last Man* (1826) is not clear: what is certain is that 'The Masque of the Red Death' has influenced numerous later writers on similar themes, including most notably Jack London in *The Scarlet Plague*. Inevitably the story reflects his tortured state of mind in the wake of his wife's illness. Commenting on Poe's behaviour during this period, Graham wrote:

> His love for his wife was a sort of rapturous worship of the spirit of beauty which he felt was fading before his eyes . . . . It was the hourly *anticipation* of her loss that made him a sad and thoughtful man, and lent a mournful melody to his undying song.

'The Pit and the Pendulum' is one of the dozen or so stories which seem destined to earn for Poe a permanent niche in English literature. It possesses that nightmare quality which characterises Poe's writing at its best – indeed the present writer can testify to the power of its visual images which have remained vividly in the mind over a period of thirty years.

No one has excelled him in conveying the horror of confinement, or in describing the fear experienced by the prisoner awaiting as yet unknown evil from his tormentors:

> So far, I had not opened my eyes. I felt that I lay upon my back, unbound. I reached out my hand, and it fell heavily upon something damp and hard. There I suffered it to remain for many minutes, while I strove to imagine where and *what* I could be. I longed, yet dared not to employ my

vision. I dreaded the first glance at objects around me. It was not that I feared to look upon things horrible, but that I grew aghast lest there should be *nothing* to see. At length, with a wild desperation at heart, I quickly unclosed my eyes. My worst thoughts, then, were confirmed. The blackness of eternal night encompassed me.

With great skill Poe describes the sensations of the prisoner on awaking in the dungeon cell at Toledo. He has been sentenced to death and, on waking after a long sleep, imagines at first he is confined by the walls of a tomb. On realising that he has not, after all, been buried alive he proceeds to a detailed examination of the dungeon. Since he is in complete darkness the narrator does not know the shape or the dimensions of his cell but he resolves to ascertain this by carefully walking around the walls, groping his way inch by inch through the inky blackness. Poe's craftsmanship as a writer is such that, at each stage of the narrator's experiences, the reader shares with him his sensations of horror and suspense. The reader can almost *feel* the slimy coldness of the dungeon walls, the treacherous surface of the floor, the terrifying awareness that at any moment the inquisitors may introduce some unseen form of torture. The prisoner's horror is complete on learning that in the centre of the dungeon is a circular pit of unknown depth, from which emerges 'the peculiar smell of decayed fungus'.

At this point in the narrative, which is written throughout in • the vivid circumstantial manner Poe had derived from Defoe and others, the prisoner falls into a drugged sleep. On awaking, he finds that he is bound painfully to a wooden framework and that immediately above him is a painted figure of Father Time bearing, instead of a scythe, a huge crescent of shining steel. With uncontrollable terror he describes his emotions on realising that the crescent has a razor-sharp edge and that it is gradually descending, with a relentless hissing motion, towards his body. Poe was a master of horror and it is doubtful if, in the whole corpus of his work, he ever excelled the description of the remorseless descent of the pendulum and the helpless feelings of the prisoner watching the almost imperceptible advance. The situation has all the elements one associates with a nightmare, for not only is the narrator powerless to do anything except watch, but there seems to be no escape from his inevitable end.

With considerable ingenuity he at last alights on a method of freeing himself from his bonds, and here again, as he smears a fragment of meat over his bandages in the hope that the teeth of the rats (with which the cell is swarming) will loosen them, the reader is one with his sensations of unspeakable terror:

> They pressed – they swarmed upon **me** in ever accumulating heaps. They writhed upon my **thr**oat; their cold lips sought my own; I was half stifled by their thronging pressure; disgust, for which the world **has** no name, swelled my bosom, and chilled, with a heavy clamminess, my heart.

When the teeth of the hungry rats loosen the surcingle and the prisoner steps free, the pendulum is at once drawn upwards through the ceiling and he realises that his every movement has been watched by his unseen tormentors. A final horror now awaits him, for the iron walls of the dungeon are heated to an unbearable temperature and then begin to close in, so that he is forced irresistibly towards the loathsome pit. With a rumbling sound the walls advance as he approaches nearer and nearer to the rat-infested well. In a final paragraph – a very contrived piece of writing, as if Poe is over-anxious to press the story to an abrupt conclusion – we learn that the French army has entered Toledo and that 'the Inquisition was in the hands of its enemies'. With this rather implausible anti-climax, in which the hero is saved from the pit at the very last moment by the outstretched hand of General Lasalle, Poe brings to an end one of his most gripping and carefully-structured tales.

We need not quarry 'The Pit and the Pendulum' for subtle allegorical meanings. Whatever symbolic overtones may lie concealed within its framework we know enough of Poe's personal and public life at this time to be aware that the nightmarish relentlessness of his vision was cruelly apposite to himself. Worried to distraction by his wife's illness, struggling to bring together a collected edition of his works (for which he projected the title *Phantasy Pieces*), striving continually for literary recognition whilst, as always, chronically short of money, it must have seemed to Poe that life was one long struggle against adversity. Faced with such grim circumstances – in June 1842 he confided to a friend 'The renewed and hopeless illness of my wife, ill health on my own part, and pecuniary embarrassments, have nearly driven me to distraction.' – the wonder is that he succeeded in producing any creative writing at all, let alone work of enduring literary merit. He was, then, caught himself between 'the pit and the pendulum': between the pendulum of financial adversity and the pit of degradation and death. A grim choice indeed, and one which he faced throughout almost all his working life.

Poe had probably read Juan Antonio Llorente's *Critical History of the Spanish Inquisition* and it is possible that some details of the setting may be derived from this work; for the rest he relied on his own fertile imagination. The story remains unsurpassed as a study in unbearable suspense and as a supreme example of a genre in which, by an accumulation of circumstantial detail, the author succeeds in creating a single unforgettable image.

F. O. C. Darley, an artist friend of Poe's, described many years later how the author read to him the manuscript of 'The Black Cat':

> The form of Poe's manuscripts was peculiar. He wrote on half sheets of notepaper, which he pasted together at the ends, making one continuous piece, which he rolled up tightly. As he read he dropped it upon the floor. It was very neatly written and without corrections apparently.[11]

The cat was Poe's favourite animal and for some years a pet cat, Catarina, was a much loved member of his household, accompanying him on his various removals. In 'The Black Cat' he created a weird fantasia embodying his affection for these animals and his fear of his violent outbursts of temper when affected by alcohol. The narrator in this story presents himself as a kindly, docile man who has always been notable for his fondness of animals. In a fit of range after a drinking bout he first gouges the eye out of a beloved cat, Pluto; then, a few days later, hangs it; finally murdering his wife with an axe and confessing his crime to the authorities. Throughout this bizarre narrative – which the storyteller describes as 'most wild, yet most homely' – the narrator insists on his rationality and humanity, asserting that his undoing was 'the spirit of *perverseness*. Of this spirit philosophy takes no account. Yet I am not more sure that my soul lives, than I am that perverseness is one of the primitive impulses of the human heart – one of the indivisible primary faculties, or sentiments, which give direction to the character of Man'. Consciously or unconsciously Poe was expressing in this tale his fear that his fits of temper might hurt those he cared for most in the world, Virginia and Maria Clemm, Sober, he knew that he was courteous and refined at all times; he also knew that when in an alcoholic rage rationality deserted him. It is this factor – the ability to lay bare his own inner contradictions and weaknesses in fictional form – which gives to his tales their unusual quality. Many of his stories have this dual nature: the dispassionate reasonableness of the narrator or central character, contrasted with the violent and terrible behaviour which is so methodically described. In other writers the act of calmly writing down the descriptions of irrational events is in most instances therapeutic, but this does not seem to have been so in Poe's case. He remained throughout his working life a deeply divided man, prone to fits of depression and oblivion and yet capable of sustained intellectual effort and of viewing his own weaknesses with detachment and candour.

    Closely linked with 'The Black Cat' in mood and form is 'The Tell-Tale Heart'. This piece, rejected by the editor of the Boston *Miscellany*, was published in the first issue of James Russell Lowell's new magazine, *The Pioneer* (January 1843). Here the narrator again protests his sanity but reveals his deranged mind by the fevered nervousness of his language and the total irrationality of the story he unfolds. It is a detailed account of the coldblooded murder of an old man, a murder committed for no other motive than that the victim has 'the eye of a vulture – a pale blue eye, with a film over it'. The murderer buries the dismembered body beneath the floorboards of the chamber, but is haunted by the continual sound of a heartbeat: this he ascribes to the old man but it is in reality the sound of his own heart exaggerated by excitement and fear. When police officers carry out a search of the building, suspecting foul play, the murderer is driven to a torment of horror by the remorseless beating of the heart until at last he can contain himself no longer and confesses to his crime. Similarly the narrator of 'The Black Cat' is forced to reveal the murder of his wife by the howling of the animal he has walled up within the tomb.

There is some evidence that Poe suffered from heart disease during the latter years of his life, probably from 1842 onwards,[12] and 'The Tell-Tale Heart' may well be in one sense an imaginative interpretation of his own fears of disease. Some critics also detect in the tale signs of Poe's growing fear of insanity under the long drawn out strain of Virginia's illness. The story is perhaps of most interest today as a case study of a certain type of criminal mentality, that of the man who is capable of planning and executing a murder with meticulous care and yet in other directions is manifestly unbalanced and incapable of giving a rational account of his own actions. As a study in the psychology of the criminal persona 'The Tell-Tale Heart' could not be bettered. To contemporary readers such stories must have seemed the product of a disordered brain, but to our own neurotic age, with our knowledge of the deep wells of fear and darkness in the human unconscious, his wildest fictions strike an answering chord.

'The Oblong Box' is one of Poe's least known stories. It has received remarkably little critical attention and is not included in many collections of his work, yet it is one of the most carefully executed of his short tales and merits close attention for its workmanship and symmetry of construction. The opening sentences, in Poe's most assured and finished manner, at once arouse the reader's attention and set the tone for the circumstantial account which is to follow:

> Some years ago, I engaged passage from Charleston, S.C., [South Carolina] to the city of New York, in the fine packet-ship 'Independence', Captain Hardy. We were to sail on the fifteenth of the month (June), weather permitting; and, on the fourteenth, I went on board to arrange some matters in my state-room.

The narrator goes on to explain that among the passengers he found several acquaintances, including a former student friend, Cornelius Wyatt. He observes that Wyatt is accompanied by two sisters, by a lady who purports to be his wife, and by an oblong pine box from which Wyatt refuses to be parted. During the voyage he is struck by his friend's moroseness and by the fact that Wyatt shuts himself away in his state-room, leaving his wife to her own devices. The narrator observes that the behaviour of his old acquaintance becomes more and more curious as the voyage proceeds; he evidently has a horror of any mention of the mysterious box, he and his wife occupy separate apartments but attempt to conceal this fact from the other passengers, and, strangest of all, he is apparently in the habit of opening the box each night and gazing at the contents, sobbing whilst doing so.

A vividly written account of a storm at sea then follows, in which Poe makes excellent use of the sea lore he must have picked up whilst stationed near Charleston during his service in the United States army. (He had himself sailed from Boston to Charleston in the fall of 1827, the voyage down the coast taking eleven days, and during his sojourn in Carolina he acquired many impressions of scenery and atmosphere which he later put to good use in 'The Gold-Bug', 'The Oblong Box' and his poetry.) When it becomes evident that the storm is so serious that the ship will have to be abandoned, Wyatt pleads with the captain to save the oblong box, but the captain refuses. Wyatt then springs from the jolly-boat on to the wrecked "Independence", ties himself to the precious box, then flings both himself and the box into the sea. A month later, having recovered from the shipwreck and other privations, the narrator chances to meet Captain Hardy in New York. The captain then reveals the solution to the mystery. Wyatt's wife, it transpires, had died at the commencement of the voyage. The young husband, beside himself with grief, had resolved to take the corpse to her mother, but in order not to arouse alarm had had the body partially embalmed and passed the box off as merchandise. His wife's maid had then impersonated the deceased lady so as to avoid any mention of the death during the voyage.

What distinguishes the tale is Poe's facility in constructing such a taut and convincing narrative hinging upon a single, simple idea – a facility to which any summary fails to do justice. Indeed the story possesses all the ingredients which one associates with the short story at its best, and which are accepted as commonplace amongst later examples of the genre. There is, first, the circumstantial opening paragraph, written in the first person and calculated to engage the reader's interest from the outset. Then the leisured, matter-of-fact narrative in which detail is carefully added to detail to build up a composite whole, whilst avoiding at this stage any *éclaircissement*. Then finally the full and detailed explanation in which the problem is elucidated and all loose ends neatly tied up. That these elements are taken for granted today strengthens rather than diminishes Poe's achievement. The literary devices employed by Poe have since been employed by many writers almost as a stock in trade; it is important to remember that in the 1840s such techniques were new and novel. The short story as an art form was still in process of gestation, and his contribution to its development was, as we shall see, very considerable.

The story concludes with the following memorable passage:

But of late, it is a rare thing that I sleep soundly at night. There is a countenance which haunts me, turn as I will. There is an hysterical laugh which will forever ring within my ears.

It is interesting to compare this with the closing words of Stevenson's *Treasure Island*:

Oxen and wain-ropes would not bring me back again to that accursed island; and the worst dreams that ever I have are when I hear the surf booming about its coasts or start upright in bed, with the sharp voice of Captain Flint still ringing in my ears: 'Pieces of eight! pieces of eight!'

Or, again, with the penultimate paragraph of Wells's *The War of the Worlds*:

Of a night I see the black powder darkening the silent streets, and the contorted bodies shrouded in that layer; they rise upon me tattered and dog-bitten. They gibber and grow fiercer, paler, uglier, mad distortions of humanity at last, and I wake, cold and wretched, in the darkness of the night.

Clearly Poe as a short story writer exercised an influence upon many subsequent writers including figures as diverse as Wells, Kafka, Conan Doyle and Algernon Blackwood, but 'The Oblong Box' is of particular relevance to any discussion of Poe as an exemplar because of its palpable literary qualities. It relies on no sensational effects or gothic trappings but simply on its narrative properties, and in this it surely represents its author at the summit of his powers.

For some time Poe had been interested in mesmerism and its possibilities. In 1844 his quasi-scientific essay 'Mesmeric Revelation' was published and aroused such interest that it was widely reprinted. He had been much influenced by the Rev. C. H. Townshend's *Facts in Mesmerism* (London, 1840) and by the possibility of deducing information concerning life and death from mesmeric experiments. Although he was not a spiritualist – in July 1844 he wrote to James Russell Lowell saying 'I have no belief in spirituality. I think the word a *mere* word. No one has really a conception of spirit. We cannot imagine what is not.'[13] – he was fascinated by such concepts as immortality and the implications of hypnotism upon an understanding of man's fundamental nature. In December 1845 he followed 'Mesmeric Revelation' with a short story which quickly became a *cause célèbre*, 'The Facts in the Case of M. Valdemar'. This tale, purporting to be a factual account of a man dying under hypnosis whose corpse is then preserved for seven months, enjoyed a considerable vogue in both Britain and the United States. In England it was even reprinted as a pamphlet bearing the impressive title *Mesmerism 'In Articulo Mortis'. An Astounding and Horrifying Narration Shewing the extraordinary power of Mesmerism in arresting the Progress of Death* and was also published in the London *Morning Post*. So generally was the story accepted as a scientific description of an actual event that Poe felt obliged to reply to correspondents with a disclaimer. '"Hoax" *is* precisely the word suited to M. Valdemar's case', he wrote to a Scottish enquirer, 'Some few persons believe it – but *I* do not – and don't you.'

The story has been described as 'the most tasteless and disgusting tale Edgar ever wrote'[14] and certainly the final paragraphs, with their account of the instant putrefaction of the body leaving 'upon the bed, before that whole company.... a nearly liquid mass of loathsome – of detestable putridity' are not recommended reading for the squeamish. The interest of the story today lies perhaps less in its theme, which is admittedly gruesome, than in the literary techniques employed by Poe to achieve his effects. Notice, firstly, the detailed description of Valdemar himself:

> M. Valdemar, who has resided principally at Harlaem, N.Y., since the year 1839, is (or was) particularly noticeable for the extreme spareness of his person – his lower limbs much resembling those of John Randolph; and, also, for the whiteness of his whiskers, in violent contrast to the blackness of his hair – the latter, in consequence, being very generally mistaken for a wig.

No one reading this account could possibly doubt that Valdemar was a real person. Poe adds a number of convincing details, including the titles of several books compiled or edited by Valdemar and particulars of his temperament. This forms the prelude to a methodical and wholly dispassionate account of his subject's illness and subsequent demise, a description calling for all Poe's skill in narrating the most horrendous details with clinical impartiality. Verisimilitude is added to the story by the frequent introduction of circumstantial detail – the naming of individuals, dialogues with Valdemar whilst under hypnosis, descriptions of the patient's symptoms, the reactions of witnesses in the bedchamber – and so on. Throughout all the sensational minutiæ of the tale the author maintains a pose of scientific calm; at several stages in the narrative he admits that the events being recounted in such a matter of fact way may strain the reader's credulity, but states that it is his duty to describe the facts to the best of his ability. (The following sentence, towards the end of the narrative, is an excellent example of Poe's technique: 'I now feel that I have reached a point of this narrative at which every reader will be startled into positive disbelief. It is my business, however, simply to proceed.') This pose of studied veracity, an apparent desire to tell the truth regardless of the consequences and of the feelings of his readers, must have contributed substantially to the widespread acceptance of the story as a piece of factual reportage. The device has since been widely emulated by other writers, most notably by H. G. Wells in such short stories as 'The Story of the Late Mr. Elvesham', 'The Sea Raiders' and 'The Remarkable Case of Davidson's Eyes'. In such tales as 'Valdemar' and 'The Premature Burial' Poe was not simply giving imaginative expression to his interest in hypnotism and the corruption of the flesh but was exploiting, through fiction, his and his readers' curiosity on a range of scientific and philosophical ideas topical at the outset of the Victorian age. That the stories have worn so well, despite their grisly theme, is a tribute to the sheer power of their author in creating an atmosphere of sustained and unforgettable horror.

Towards the end of his short life Poe began to be overwhelmed by illness and frustration. All his life he had sought acceptance as a man of letters but literary recognition in the form in which he desired it continually eluded him. His efforts to become owner and editor of a literary journal which would set the highest critical standards came to nought, although he never gave up trying. (His last fateful journey to Philadelphia and Baltimore in September and October 1849 was to raise funds for a projected new magazine.) Similarly his attempts to interest publishers in a collected edition of his works which would demonstrate the full range of his talents were frustrated time and again, though this too was a project he revived at intervals over a period of many years. Tired, ill and depressed, Poe gave vent to his frustration in two stories of revenge, 'The Cask of Amontillado' and 'Hop-Frog', both of which reveal much concerning Poe's state of mind during the closing years of his life.

'The Cask of Amontillado', published in *Godey's Lady's Book* in November 1846, is a masterly tale of retribution. Fortunato, a connoisseur of wine, is lured into the catacombs of the Montresor family by his enemy Montresor, ostensibly to sample a cask of Amontillado sherry. Fortunato is led into a remote part of the crypt and then, whilst under the influence of wine (for it is the carnival season, and he has been drinking much) he is fettered to the granite by his murderer and then walled up in the catacomb.

I thrust a torch through the remaining aperture and let it fall within. There came forth in return only a jingling of the bells. My heart grew sick; it was the dampness of the catacombs that made it so. I hastened to make an end of my labour. I forced the last stone into its position; I plastered it up. Against the new masonry I re-erected the old rampart of bones. For the half of a century no mortal has disturbed them. *In pace requiescat!*

Apart from its intrinsic qualities – the skill with which Poe, in the minimum of words, conveys the animosity between the two protagonists; the unforgettable description of the vaults, encrusted with nitre; the motif of revenge which is present throughout the story (the motto of the Montresors is 'Nemo me impune lacessit' ['no one provokes me with impunity']); the remorseless manner in which Fortunato's incarceration is both achieved and described – the story embodies some of Poe's most characteristic preoccupations. Burial alive, a theme previously treated in 'The Black Cat' and 'The Premature Burial', here receives an additional dimension of horror for it is combined with the idea of punishment. One feels with Montresor for having borne 'the thousand injuries of Fortunato', and the reader is at one with him in sensing that Fortunato receives his deserts. Whether the story is read as an allegory on the eternal conflict between the unimaginative man and the creative artist, or simply as a self-portrait of two aspects of Poe himself, 'The Cask of Amontillado' remains one of his most brilliantly written tales and one which deserves to be included in any anthology of horror.

'Hop-Frog', written in February 1849 (eight months before his death) is a darker parable on human follies. The Hop-Frog of the story is a court jester, a dwarf, who is in love with a girl, Trippetta. The jester has distorted legs and can only walk with great difficulty, a fact which 'afforded illimitable amusement, and of course consolation, to the king'. During a masquerade the king demands that Hop-Frog shall produce an idea for some agreeable diversion involving fancy dress. The dwarf, maddened with the king for having insulted his beloved, suggests that the king and his seven ministers shall dress as the Eight Chained Orang-Outangs. The eight are first encased in tights, then tarred and covered with a thick coating of flax so as to resemble apes; they are then chained together. The jester then wreaks his revenge on the hated king by setting him and his ministers alight with a flambeau. Shouting to the assembled company that *'this is my last jest'* Hop-Frog, together with Trippetta, makes his escape.

Owing to the high combustibility of both the flax and the tar to which it adhered, the dwarf had scarcely made an end of his brief speech before the work of vengeance was complete. The eight corpses swung in their chains, a fetid, blackened, hideous, and indistinguishable mass. The cripple hurled his torch at them, clambered leisurely to the ceiling, and disappeared through the sky-light.

This is a powerful piece of writing which must have been written in a white heat of anger and unhappiness. It was written while Poe was still tormented by the death of his young wife and by twenty years of humiliation and penury at the hands of editors and publishers, some of whom had profited greatly by his work. During the winter of 1848–9 he had worn himself out writing, rewriting, and corresponding far and wide in pursuit of his El Dorado of critical success. Medical evidence suggests that during this period the condition of his heart was deteriorating and that he was probably also suffering from mental illness. Moreover the story was conceived immediately after his offer of marriage had been rejected by Mrs. Whitman and he had experienced a wounding rebuff by her and her family. Filled with bitterness at the apparent failure of his life and unable to exact retribution upon those who had caused him so many humiliations, he took his revenge, symbolically and imaginatively, through his fiction.

As always with Poe, the story is capable of interpretation on a number of different levels. On the one hand it can be read as a straightforward exercise in horror, a tale of revenge on a par with Wells's 'The Cone' or Conan Doyle's 'The Case of Lady Sannox'. On a deeper level it can be interpreted as a powerful allegory: the king representing Reality, the eternal antagonist of the creative mind, and the jester representing Imagination, the creative artist who is maimed and imprisoned by the unthinking majority. However one chooses to interpret Poe's intentions there can be no question that 'Hop-Frog' was written with deep emotion and resentment: it is a cry of despair in which the bottled up resentment of a lifetime found expression.

TALES OF RATIOCINATION

Poe is rightly credited with the invention of the short tale of detection as a literary form and with the creation of the abstract, analytical reasoner which subsequently became the model for such detectives as Sherlock Holmes and Solar Pons. His first exercise in this manner was 'Maelzel's Chess-Player' (1836) in which he demonstrated by a process of methodical reasoning that an automaton chess-player then travelling round American cities was in reality operated by a concealed man. This attracted widespread attention at the time and foreshadowed the methods of deductive reasoning he was later to employ in the stories featuring C. Auguste Dupin.

The first of these, 'The Murders in the Rue Morgue', was written at a period when he was becoming more and more interested in the idea of solving crimes by a process of logic. During his spell as assistant editor of *Burton's Gentleman's Magazine* he had read a series of articles entitled 'Unpublished Passages in the Life of Vidocq, the French Minister of Police' and had been struck by the crudity of contemporary police methods and their heavy reliance upon circumstantial evidence. He had no reason to believe that the methods employed by American police were any more sophisticated than those employed by their French counterparts, and moreover American newspapers at the time were filled with reports of sensational crimes and murder trials. Poe determined to try his hand at composing a fictional narrative in which an apparently inexplicable murder would be solved by the application of pure reason. This time the story was set neither in the United States nor in England but in Paris, a city which, as far as is known, he had never visited.

Dupin is presented as a 'young gentleman of an excellent –
indeed of an illustrious family' who has been reduced to
poverty but has a small independent income. The narrator
befriends him and the two decide to share the same apartments. The narrator illustrates Dupin's remarkable powers of
deduction by describing an incident in which Dupin follows
his mental processes over a period of fifteen minutes, reasoning correctly from cause to effect (a feat replicated by Sherlock
Holmes in 'The Resident Patient', who reminds Watson that
'some little time ago when I read you a passage in one of Poe's
sketches, in which a close reasoner follows the unspoken
thoughts of his companion, you were inclined to treat the
matter as a mere *tour de force* of the author.'

The story itself – in which a mother and daughter are
found brutally and inexplicably murdered, and are later
found to have been killed by an orang-outang – is remarkable
for its originality. The basic ingredients of the crime were no
doubt gathered by Poe from a variety of sources: the idea of an
outrage committed by an ape may have been suggested to him
by contemporary newspaper reports, whilst the device of a
murder committed in a locked room appears to have been
derived from Scott's novel *Count Robert of Paris*. What is novel
in the story is Poe's whole approach to the mystery and its
ultimate solution. The reader is first presented with a detailed
account of the crime in the form of verbatim reports from
newspapers; this account includes statements made by friends
and neighbours of the deceased and by others who heard
suspicious sounds emanating from the death chamber. This is
followed by Dupin's own on-the-spot investigation in the
course of which the detective minutely analyses the elements
of the mystery in conversation with his friend. The narrative
culminates in the apprehension of the owner of the orang-
outang (Dupin having hit on the idea of advertising for the
owner to come forward and claim the animal from his
address) and a full explanation of all aspects of the problem.

The central principle of the science of deduction is expressed by Dupin in these terms: 'They [the Police] have fallen
into the gross but common error of confounding the unusual
with the abstruse. But it is by these deviations from the plane of
the ordinary, that reason feels its way, if at all, in its search for
the true.' Reasoning in a calm, methodical, step by step manner,

Dupin succeeds in solving a crime of atrocious violence – a murder which the authorities had found baffling in its apparent absence of motive or clues – and in doing so paved the way for a host of later detectives, many modelled frankly on his example. The brilliant stories of Sir Arthur Conan Doyle (see especially 'The Abbey Grange' and 'Black Peter' as examples of the genre) and of Dorothy L. Sayers, to name but two, plainly owe much to Dupin and to the rationale of the detective story as adumbrated by Poe. There had of course been stories involving crime and detection prior to 1841: such narratives as William Godwin's *Caleb Williams* (1794) and Bulwer Lytton's *Eugene Aram* (1832) come to mind, but Poe was the first to write an analytical detective story in which the hero solves a crime solely by deduction and the application of disinterested logic. In writing 'The Murders in the Rue Morgue' he was giving birth to a branch of literature which has provided (and continues to provide) entertainment and pleasure for millions of readers. His techniques and methodology have been adapted and refined by many of the writers who came after him, but they have not been superseded.

In February 1841 Poe wrote a review of *Barnaby Rudge* (then appearing serially in the United States) in which he not only predicted the outcome of the story but even analysed Dickens's thought processes with remarkable acumen. So accurate was his diagnosis that Dickens is said to have exclaimed 'the man must be the devil'. When the mood took him Poe undoubtedly excelled at the methodical and minutely detailed examination of facts, and following the publication of 'The Murders in the Rue Morgue' he cast about for some other theme which would serve as a medium for Dupin's impressive powers of deduction. He found it in an actual murder case, the brutal killing of a young girl in New York in the year 1842. Writing to his friend Dr. J. E. Snodgrass in June of that year he explained:

> The story is based upon that of the real murder of Mary Cecilia Rogers, which created so vast an excitement some months ago in New York. I have handled the design in a very singular and entirely *novel* manner . . . . In fact, I really believe, not only that I have demonstrated the falsity of the

idea that the girl was the victim of a gang, but have indicated *the assassin*. My main object, however . . . . is the analysis of the *principles of investigation* in cases of like character. Dupin *reasons* the matter throughout.

In this story, 'The Mystery of Marie Rogêt', Poe closely paralleled the details of the actual murder, as reported in the New York press, but for the purposes of the narrative changed the names of individuals and locations and transplanted the events once again to Paris. The story affords a remarkable and sustained example of the way in which an apparently insoluble problem can be resolved by the relentless application of reason to all its component elements. By a minute examination and analysis of newspaper reports bearing on the mystery, Dupin is able to demonstrate the inconsistency and fallaciousness of many of the published accounts of the crime; the superficial nature of the police enquiries; the heavy reliance by the authorities upon tacit or unverified assumptions; the failure of the authorities to employ strictly *scientific* methods of investigation; and the fundamental error of the official theory that the murdered girl had been the victim of a gang attack instead of a single assassin.

To a perceptive reader not the least interesting feature of these Dupin stories – apart from the fascinating minutiae of crime detection itself (of which perhaps the most celebrated examples in our own century are the many investigations into the assassination of President Kennedy) – is the deft manner with which Poe rounds and completes his portrait of Dupin. Throughout these tales of ratiocination Poe introduces human touches which serve to strengthen our impression of Dupin, not simply as a cool, dispassionate thinking machine but as an idiosyncratic human being. We learn, for example, that 'It was a freak of fancy in my friend . . . . to be enamoured of the Night for her own sake', and that he and his colleague would frequently sally forth into the streets at night-time in search of interest and excitement. We learn, too, that 'Upon the winding up of the tragedy involved in the deaths of Madam L'Espanaye and her daughter, ['The Murders in the Rue Morgue'] the Chevalier dismissed the affair at once from his attention, and relapsed into his old habits of moody reverie.' It is touches such as these, so widely emulated by the writers who followed him, which give the illusion of verisimilitude to these pioneer detective stories.

Poe was right to stress that he had 'handled the design in a very singular and entirely *novel* manner'. Again and again in these narratives, not least in 'Marie Rogêt', one is impressed with his intellectual powers and his ability to sift through a bewildering array of conflicting evidence by the application of reason alone. Unquestionably in his private life there were phases of mental illness, periods in which he departed altogether from that cool, calm rationality so highly regarded by Dupin. Some critics have seen in this evidence that Poe was creating a compensating personality, that in creating Dupin he was deliberately giving fictional expression to an idealisation of himself. What is not in doubt is that in inventing Dupin and giving him a series of baffling crimes to investigate and solve Poe was giving birth to a new literary form which was to become one of the most potent in our culture.

'The Mystery of Marie Rogêt' has never attained the popularity of the other stories featuring C. Auguste Dupin, partly because of its excessively complicated plot – to follow all the intricacies of the drama and of Dupin's deductive processes requires an effort of concentration beyond the reach of many readers – and partly because of its length (the story is considerably longer than 'The Gold-Bug' and could almost be regarded as a novella). Poe deserves credit, however, for having deliberately chosen to investigate a real crime under the guise of fiction: a courageous thing to do at any time but especially in the America of the 1840s. To pursue the truth regardless of the consequences and motivated solely by a desire to establish the facts was both honourable and novel in his day. The story has earned for itself a respected place in the history of detective fiction and one which helped to enhance both Poe's reputation as an analytical thinker and Dupin's renown as the infallible solver of intractable problems.

'The Purloined Letter,' the third and last of the Dupin stories, is the shortest of the three but possibly the one which has been most influential in shaping the rationale of the detective story as we know it today. The opening paragraph, for example, might almost be taken for the beginning of any Sherlock Holmes story:

At Paris, just after dark one gusty evening in the autumn of 18————, I was enjoying the twofold luxury of meditation and a meerschaum, in company with my friend . . . .. For one hour at least we had maintained a profound silence; while each, to any casual observer, might have seemed intently and exclusively occupied with the curling eddies of smoke that oppressed the atmosphere of the chamber.

These preliminary sentences, so redolent of an atmosphere of thought and reflection, form the backcloth to one of the most intriguing mysteries Dupin has been called upon to investigate. A letter containing information of a highly delicate nature has been stolen from the royal apartments. The problem is to recover the letter from the thief, a government Minister, before the information contained in the document can be put to illegitimate use. The police authorities have carried out a minutely thorough search of the thief's apartments but their utmost efforts have failed to find any trace of the missing letter. The Prefect of police explains the problem to Dupin who, a month later, and much to the Prefect's astonishment, produces the elusive letter in return for a cheque for 50,000 francs. Dupin has once again arrived at a solution to the problem simply by the unremitting application of reason. Reasoning that the thief would expect the police to find the letter *concealed* and that he has therefore confounded them by *not* concealing it, Dupin acts upon this assumption. He visits the Minister in his chambers and, after a careful scrutiny of the room, finds the letter in a card-rack where it has been placed with apparent casualness by the thief. The card-rack being fully open to view, and the letter having been deliberately soiled and crumpled by the cunning Minister, it had failed to arouse the attention of the authorities, who had acted throughout on the mistaken belief that the document would be carefully hidden. Thus Dupin is able to fathom the riddle, simply by a process of deduction stemming from his knowledge of the 'daring, dashing, and discriminating ingenuity' of the thief.

Artistically 'The Purloined Letter' is the finest of Poe's tales of detection, although it has been outshone by the more sensational 'Murders in the Rue Morgue'. The later story contains no violent crimes or dramatic set-pieces but relies for its effects on other, less outré elements: the skilful building up of an atmosphere conducive to calm analysis, the methodical unfolding of an apparently impenetrable mystery, the surprise solution, and finally the step by step revelation of the deductive processes leading up to the conclusion. Poe organises and handles his material with complete mastery throughout. Dupin is at his brilliant best, the conversations between him and his friend are dexterously wrought, and the relationship between the two protagonists and the Prefect is achieved with great subtlety. Poe was a fastidious craftsman, and one imagines him revising and re-revising the story until he was absolutely satisfied with it as a work of art.

The influence of 'The Purloined Letter' upon the literature of crime detection has been profound. This can be seen not only in the work of Conan Doyle (see especially 'The Naval Treaty' and 'A Scandal in Bohemia') but in the stories of writers as diverse as G. K. Chesterton, Dorothy L. Sayers and Ellery Queen. With the publication of the three Dupin stories during the years 1841–5, Poe established for all time the conventions of the genre which have been followed to greater or lesser extent by all subsequent crime writers: the brilliant but eccentric detective who possesses uncanny reasoning powers, and who subordinates all else to his intellectual gifts; the devoted but less intelligent friend; the puzzling crime which defeats the utmost efforts of the police; the innocent suspect; and finally the detailed explanation by the detective and the complete solution of the mystery. Conan Doyle acknowledged that any writer who sought to emulate Poe in this field was left 'with no fresh ground they can confidently call their own'.

In 1843 Poe learned that the Philadelphia *Dollar Newspaper* was offering a prize of 100 dollars for the best short story submitted under the terms of a contest. He decided to enter his story 'The Gold-Bug' (originally written a year earlier for publication in his projected magazine *The Stylus*); to his delight the committee of judges awarded him the prize. As a result not only was 'The Gold-Bug' printed and reprinted in the *Dollar Newspaper* but it attracted widespread critical and popular attention. The story quickly became one of his most celebrated tales.

The popularity of the story is due principally to its undoubted literary qualities – there can be no doubt that he took immense pains over the writing of it and continued to revise it even after its first publication – and to the accomplished way in which Poe blended a number of classic ingredients of the romantic adventure story: buried treasure, a secret code, a long buried chart, a lonely island and the unravelling of a recondite mystery. That he was well versed in the lore of pirates and hidden gold there can be no question. Charleston and its surrounding coast which he knew intimately from his army days, was teeming with stories of pirates and had associations with such infamous names as Black Beard and Steede Bonnet. A few years earlier he had reviewed *Sheppard Lee* by Robert M. Bird, an exciting tale in which the hero embarks on a search for Captain Kidd's buried treasure. The combination of these elements, coupled with the solving of a cryptogram, had an irresistible appeal for Poe, who never forgot the delights of his boyhood reading. In an article written in 1836 for the *Southern Literary Messenger* he wrote:

> How fondly do we recur in memory to those enchanted days when we first learned to grow serious over Robinson Crusoe! – when we first found the spirit of wild adventure enkindling within us, as by the dim firelight we laboured out, line by line, the marvellous import of those pages, and hung breathless and trembling with eagerness over their absorbing – over their enchanting interest. Alas! the days of desolate islands are no more.

Sullivan's Island, described so vividly in 'The Gold-Bug', was a location he knew very well indeed, for he was stationed there (at Fort Moultrie, a few miles from Charleston) during 1827–8 and during his spell there became closely familiar with the island and its curious natural history. Dr. Edmund Ravenel, a naturalist who lived on the island, may have been the inspiration for the 'William Legrand' of the story; certainly he befriended Poe and the two of them, sometimes together and sometimes alone, spent hours wandering over its lonely scrub forests and desolate beaches. This remote terrain clearly exercised a powerful effect on his imagination, and it is remarkable that the details of the scenery remained impressed on his mind until the story came to be written fourteen years later. The island, as described by Poe at the beginning of the story, is as haunting and unforgettable as that described in Stevenson's *Treasure Island* or Wells's *The Island of Doctor Moreau*:

This island is a very singular one. It consists of little else than the sea-sand, and is about three miles long. Its breadth at no point exceeds a quarter of a mile. It is separated from the mainland by a scarcely perceptible creek, oozing its way through a wilderness of reeds and slime, a favourite resort of the marsh-hen. The vegetation, as might be supposed, is scant, or at least dwarfish.... the whole island.... is covered with a dense undergrowth of the sweet myrtle so much prized by the horticulturists of England.

It is in this melancholy setting that the narrator encounters William Legrand, a man after Poe's heart – well educated, bookish, and with a marked taste for solitude. With considerable mastery Legrand and his menage are described and the reader is introduced to Legrand's negro servant, Jupiter, one of the most vivid and well drawn characters Poe ever created. The 'gold-bug' itself which plays such a prominent part in the story and which is described with such particularity is an amalgam of two beetles actually found on the island, *Callichroma*, the gold-bug, and *Alaus Oculatus*, the skull-bug. The synthesising of the two and the ingenious manner in which the bug is employed in the recovery of the treasure is characteristic of Poe's scientific manner and the masterly way in which he could make the implausible appear convincing. He blended into the tale besides the elements already noted – a fascination with pirate lore and secret codes, analytical expertise and a minutely observed topographical background – a lively curiosity about people and nature and a veracity of description which makes it difficult to believe one is not reading an account of actual events.

Moreover the *structure* of the story affords an extremely interesting example of a literary device new in Poe's time but which has since become almost commonplace: first, the chance encounter with the central character and a description of his milieu; then the almost immediate involvement in the cardinal events of the narrative; and finally a detailed and carefully reasoned explanation of the behaviour of the hero and the loose ends incidental to his actions.

The principal interest of the story as a tale of ratiocination lies in the extremely skilful and painstaking manner with which Legrand proceeds to solve the mystery of the crypto-gram and thus recover the lost treasure. Poe had long been interested in secret codes and frequently invited his readers to submit cyphers to him for solution. The particular code used in 'The Gold-Bug' is of a comparatively simple nature (as Legrand himself is quick to point out) but its interest lies in the wholly ingenious manner of its solution – subsequently adopted by many other writers, including most notably Conan Doyle in 'The Dancing Men'. The detailed analysis of the frequency with which letters occur in the English language is said to have influenced Samuel Morse in the invention of Morse code.

The procedure adopted by Legrand follows an orderly and analytical pattern: (a) the crucial discovery of the death's-head drawn upon the scrap of parchment, and the realisation that it *is* parchment and not paper; (b) the heating of the parchment in order to reveal the writing in invisible ink; (c) the decoding of the cypher into English; (d) the methodical solution of the message thus revealed – this forms one of the finest sections of the entire story, and is an excellent example of the ease with which Poe could make plain apparently abstruse mysteries; and finally (e) the uncovering of the treasure, with all its concomitant excitement, and the calm elucidation of the riddle. The whole forms a remarkably sustained exercise in the art of deduction, an exercise which has profoundly influenced the short story as a genre and more particularly the tale of detection.

William Bittner, commenting on the story, has observed 'Poe was well aware that the story was hopelessly contrived; the plot was played out halfway through, and the rest is explanation, to draw the reader's attention from the basic absurdity, that Captain Kidd had gone to ridiculously melo-dramatic means to make his map secret, then had dropped it on the beach where it was fortuitously found generations later.'[15] Whilst there is some substance in this criticism it seems to the present writer to obscure an essential element in the story – that the parchment containing the mysterious cryptogram was found buried in the sand *near to the remnants of a ship's long boat*. Poe stresses that 'the wreck seemed to have been there for a very great while; for the resemblance to boat timbers could scarcely be traced'. The clear implication is that many years previously a boat containing a crew and the parchment had been wrecked off the coast of the island and subsequently washed ashore. The parchment therefore had not been merely 'dropped on the beach' but accidentally lost – to lie in the sand until discovered by Legrand generations later. (Poe was nothing if not conscientious; he was so fascinated by legends of pirates and missing treasure that, whilst in the army, he took the trouble to search through the records in the Charleston State House for details of the ship *Cid Campeador*, wrecked off the South Carolina coast in 1745).

Finally it should be noted that the story offers further evidence of that *variety* which he was constantly emphasising as a hallmark of his work. 'The Gold-Bug' possesses many of the qualities one associates with Stevenson or Conan Doyle rather than Poe, and it is not difficult to see why it has always been regarded as one of his most popular tales. It has none of the gruesome horror so many critics had disparaged in such stories as 'Valdemar' and 'The Black Cat' and is characterised throughout by writing of the highest quality. Indeed as a piece of sheer storytelling it would be difficult to fault 'The Gold-Bug' and had Poe written nothing else he would merit a place among the immortals. Not for nothing did he write 'My life has been *whim* – impulse – passion – a longing for solitude – a scorn of all things present, in an earnest desire for the future.'

TALES OF SATIRE

Poe's experiments with genres other than horror and ratiocination are little known today and are rarely included in collections of his work. Yet he devoted considerable energy to composing humorous and satirical stories in which he lampooned many of the literary and social conventions of his time. That these are little read today is partly due to changing fashions of humour – such tales as 'The Devil in the Belfry' and 'A Predicament' seem embarrassingly artificial and clumsy to modern readers – and partly because the targets of Poe's satire, the literary pundits and politicians of America a hundred and forty years ago, have long since disappeared. With the passage of time many of these satirical stories and articles have lost much of their original force and are only read in our own day by scholars and specialists. At his best, however, Poe was a satirist in the tradition of Swift and Voltaire and there are at least four stories of this kind which merit careful attention and which should be included in any overall assessment of his work. These are 'King Pest', 'Some Words with a Mummy', 'The System of Doctor Tarr and Professor Fether' and 'Mellonta Tauta'.

'King Pest, A Tale Containing an Allegory', is written in a comic style highly reminiscent of the early Dickens. (It is known that Poe was an admirer of Dickens and had read and praised *The Old Curiosity Shop* and *Barnaby Rudge*. He cannot have been influenced by Dickens as early as 1835, however (when 'King Pest' was written), as Dickens's first work, *Sketches by Boz*, was not published in the United States until 1837). It is set in London during the fourteenth century and relates the adventures of two seamen belonging to the crew of the 'Free and Easy', Hugh Tarpaulin and his companion, Legs. The two set out on a carousel through a disreputable part of the city – it is the time of the plague – and, after many wanderings, find themselves in an undertaker's shop. Seated upon coffin-trestles around a table are six grotesque figures, drinking out of human skulls. The president of this assembly announces that he is 'King Pest' and that the five weirdly dressed associates are his companions. Legs demands to know the identity of the grisly coterie; an argument ensues and the story ends with the two seamen fleeing from the room after having pushed the King through a trap-door and drowned the remainder in ale.

The entire story is written with vitriolic zest and wit. Poe clearly intended the encounter in the undertaker's shop to be something of a set-piece, and he brought to it all his expertise as a storyteller. Each character in the tale is described with a

Dickensian eye for detail and the atmosphere of medieval London is vividly conveyed. Already in this early tale there are unmistakable indications of the Poe of 'The Fall of the House of Usher':

> The paving-stones, loosened from their beds, lay in wild disorder amid the tall, rank grass, which sprang up around the feet and ankles. Fallen houses choked up the streets. The most fetid and poisonous smells everywhere prevailed; – and by the aid of that ghastly light which, even at midnight, never fails to emanate from a vapoury and pestilential atmosphere, might be discerned lying in the by-paths and alleys, or rotting in the windowless habitations, the carcass of many a nocturnal plunderer arrested by the hand of the plague in the very perpetration of his robbery.

Taken all in all, 'King Pest' is a remarkable achievement. In 1835 Poe was still a young and relatively inexperienced writer (he was then twenty-six and had just become assistant editor of *The Southern Literary Messenger* in Richmond.) It is a curious mixture of comic extravaganza and satirical burlesque, and is a first exploration of a theme he was to parody many years later – in much grimmer mood – in 'The Masque of the Red Death' and 'Hop-Frog'. The allegorical elements within the tale relate to the literary climate in which aspiring writers like Poe had to work at that time. He had been writing for eight years, had had several slim volumes of poetry published and much else rejected. Despite the immense pains he lavished on his work it must have seemed to him that he received little but discouragement and 'that, by contrast, inferior work by other writers gained undue publicity. Stung by these reflections, he composed in 'King Pest' a bitter caricature of the literary establishment of his day. On this reading, the King and his grotesque cronies represent the editors and publishers, the self-appointed arbiters of good taste who, it seemed to Poe, took it upon themselves to decide what the reading public would or would not buy. Their word was law:

> Know then that in these dominions I am monarch, and here rule with undivided empire under the title of 'King Pest the

First' . . .. As regards your demand of the business upon which we sit here in council, we might be pardoned for replying that it concerns, and concerns *alone*, our own private and regal interest, and is in no manner important to any other than ourself.

The King attempts to bully Tarpaulin and Legs into drinking a gallon each of liquor and, when they refuse to do so, orders Tarpaulin to be pushed into a cask of ale. He and Legs succeed in effecting their escape, however, but not before they have scattered and drowned the King and his associates. There is no mistaking the gusto with which this part of the tale is written: Poe evidently relished the thought of the smug literati being demoralised and defeated, and, by impli-cation, the triumph of the unfettered man of letters, the victory over bigotry by those who refused to conform to arbitrary canons of literary taste. In effect he was entering a plea for experiment and innovation in literature and for an end to 'the plague' of conformity imposed by those who controlled newspapers and journals. The story may well have been written tongue in cheek, but that it was written with deep feeling there can be no doubt.

As Poe entered his fourth decade he was becoming increas-ingly disenchanted with many features of life in the brash America of the 1840s – the facile belief that democracy was the panacea for all human ills, the unquestioning acceptance of 'Progress' in the form of more and more industrial development, the glib assumptions of much historical re-search of the time – and in a series of satirical essays he sought opportunities for expressing his disillusionment. One of the most interesting of these is 'Some Words with a Mummy', a spirited tale in which a mummy from ancient Egypt, Count Allamistakeo, is revived by means of galvanism and proceeds to converse with his nineteenth-century audience on the shallowness of their beliefs and their total ignorance of the achievements of ancient civilisation.

The story is written in the easy, flowing style which Mark Twain was later to emulate with such success[16] but which Poe rarely handled with such felicity. The opening paragraphs, in which the scene is set with engaging assurance, describe the urgent summoning of the narrator to the home of his friend Doctor Ponnonner to witness the unswathing of a mummy retrieved some years previously from a tomb near Eleithias, 'a considerable distance above Thebes on the Nile'. The excitement and eager anticipation of the assembled company are vividly described as the layers of coverings are removed and the corpse itself is revealed. It is then decided as an experiment to apply electricity to the body. To the astonishment of the onlookers the mummy reacts to the electric shock by opening its eyes and, after slowly reviving, begins to address them in Egyptian.

The idea of resuscitating a cadaver by the application of electricity held great fascination for Poe, although the notion was not original. He had himself touched upon the idea a year earlier in his essay 'The Premature Burial' and may also have read the anonymous short story 'Letter from a Revived Mummy' (New York *Evening Mirror*, 21 January 1832) in which a soldier's corpse is revived after a lapse of a hundred years by means of a galvanic battery. He was certainly familiar with Jane Webb's gothic narrative *The Mummy: A Tale of the Twenty-Second Century* (1827) in which the Mummy of Cheops is brought back to life, and very probably had read Mary Shelley's novel *Frankenstein*, a pirated edition of which was issued by his own publishers, Lea and Blanchard of Philadelphia, in 1833. Yet another influence on his work was 'Address to the Mummy in Belzoni's Exhibition' (1826) written by the English writer Horace Smith, whom Poe had already caricatured in 'Epimanes' and 'A Tale of Jerusalem'.

Yet Poe was not content merely to plagiarise (though much of the Egyptian detail which adds such conviction to the tale was culled without acknowledgement from articles in the *Encyclopaedia Americana*) but instead adapted and moulded his literary and historical materials to achieve what is on careful examination an expertly contrived satire on the pretentiousness of many contemporary attitudes. In the course of conversation with the mummy all the elements of satire are brought into play – humour, irony, sarcasm and invective – in a stinging criticism of institutions and demagogy, but it should be noted that it remains throughout a *conversation* and not simply a lecture. As the mummy proceeds to describe life as he had known it and to draw unfavourable comparisons with nineteenth-century ideas of civilisation he is continually questioned and interrupted by his audience. Poe skilfully achieves the effect of a conversazione in which attitudes and assumptions are bandied back and forth and in which there is a real interplay of minds from totally different cultures.

The most biting satire is reserved for the commentary upon politicians, and especially upon democracy as Poe had experienced it. In a scathing passage the mummy comments on universal suffrage and on 'democratic' constitutions:

> Thirteen Egyptian provinces determined all at once to be free, and to set a magnificent example to the rest of mankind. They assembled their wise men, and concocted the most ingenious constitution it is possible to conceive. For a while they managed remarkably well; only their habit of bragging was prodigious. The thing ended, however, in the consolidation of the thirteen states, with some fifteen or twenty others, in the most odious and insupportable despotism that was ever heard of upon the face of the Earth.

Throughout the story Poe introduces humorous observations on politicians and on contemporary notions of progress (e.g., 'The Count merely said that Great Movements were awfully common things in his day, and as for Progress, it was at one time quite a nuisance, but it never progressed.') and delights in deflating the faith of modern men in their achievements and technology. One of the reasons why the story has received comparatively little critical attention may be that its deceptively facetious style has masked for many readers its underlying seriousness of intent. The apparent light-heartedness of the surface narrative conceals a number of disturbing questions which tormented Poe more and more as he looked about him and speculated on the future of man. For he had no faith in human perfectibility nor in the idea of the inevitability of progress. He thought on the contrary that much effort aimed at the amelioration of man's lot was wasted and that humanity was no more happy in his day than it had been at the beginning of civilisation.[17] He would in fact have agreed enthusiastically with Wells's Time Traveller who, it will be recalled 'thought but cheerlessly of the Advancement of Mankind, and saw in the growing pile of civilisation only a foolish heaping that must inevitably fall back upon and destroy its makers in the end'. In these satirical pieces, uneven as they are, he was questioning the complacent beliefs of his contemporaries and challenging, in the face of hostility and indifference, the almost universal faith in material progress. It need hardly be added that for his pains he received little but abuse and only the most derisory financial return.

The opening paragraphs of 'The System of Doctor Tarr and Professor Fether' are cast in the style of one of his exercises in horror; indeed the description of the *Maison de Santé* (private lunatic asylum) in which the story is set is strongly reminiscent of the melancholy House of Usher:

> Through this dank and gloomy wood we rode some two miles, when the *Maison de Santé* came in view. It was a fantastic *chateau*, much dilapidated, and indeed scarcely tenantable through age and neglect. Its aspect inspired me with absolute dread, and, checking my horse, I half resolved to turn back. I soon, however, grew ashamed of my weakness, and proceeded.

The narrator describes a mental institution in the South of France which, he understands, is managed on an enlightened 'system of soothing' – that is to say, a regime in which there are no punishments and in which the inmates are permitted a considerable degree of freedom. The superintendent advises him, however, that this regime has recently been abandoned in favour of more conventional methods of treatment: the 'system of soothing' had been tried as an experiment but found to be unworkable. As the story proceeds, the narrator becomes increasingly puzzled by the eccentric behaviour of all whom he encounters at the asylum, who purport to be staff and their guests; he is forbidden permission to see any of the patients. At length, as the behaviour of his hosts at the dinner table becomes so eccentric as to be alarming, he learns the truth: a month previously the inmates had seized power, tarring and feathering the keepers and then imprisoning them in underground cells. It is only when one of the keepers succeeds in escaping and freeing the others that the real inmates are routed and order is restored. The narrator realises to his chagrin that the man who posed as the superintendent was in reality insane – he had indeed been in charge of the institution some years before but, on becoming deranged himself, had been confined as a patient.

The story is not only an interesting parable on the theme of democracy and slavery but abounds in witty phrases apropos human attitudes and foibles, e.g., 'I remembered having been informed. . . . that the southern provincialists were a peculiarly eccentric people, with a vast number of antiquated notions' (here Poe is having a sly dig at the aristocratic South, which, he felt, had first adopted and then disowned and abandoned him), and 'Upon the whole, I could not help thinking that there was much of the *bizarre* about everything I saw – but then the world is made up of all kinds of persons, with all modes of thought, and all sorts of conventional customs.' Although, as we have seen, his satirical stories have never attained the popularity of his tales of terror, in his own way Poe was equally at home in the world of allegory and parable, and 'The System of Doctor Tarr and Professor Fether' is an intriguing example of the symbolic narrative as a literary form.

It is quite possible that the tale was intended as a parody of the 'Moral Treatment' of lunatics which Dickens had apparently so admired during his visit to the United States in 1842 (and subsequently described in his *American Notes*.)[18] It is equally conceivable that Poe's asylum is a satirical caricature of that described in a story, 'The Madhouse of Palermo', which he had reviewed in the *Southern Literary Messenger* in August 1836. Whatever may be the origins of the tale, it is clear that Poe was fascinated by the treatment of the mentally unstable and by the apparently irrational compulsions which can overwhelm normal human behaviour. Here he skilfully blends these ingredients in a commentary on racial attitudes which is at once scathing and profound: violence must inevitably rebound upon those who use it indiscriminately; those who have absolute authority will inevitably become corrupted by power and degenerate into tyrants; the oppressed, driven by intolerable indignities and a desire to seek revenge on their persecutors, will in the end turn the tables on their captors. Seen in these terms the story is a striking

anticipation of themes George Orwell was to develop a
century later in *Animal Farm*.

To the student of Poe not the least interesting feature of the
story is its *structure*. The dénouement, which is calculated to
take most readers by surprise, does not come until the very
final paragraph: until this climax the reader is kept in
suspense as to the outcome, since the narrator is in doubt until
the end whether his interlocutors are sane or not. Poe,
increasingly prone to mental illness and moods of depression,
was only too well aware that the borderline between insanity
and rationality can be exceedingly fine. The *style* of 'Tarr and
Fether' is also deceptively simple; it is written throughout in
an easy, flowing manner which must in practice have cost
great pains to achieve. The story is in fact a remarkable
example of a controlled, carefully thought out and executed
narrative which is at the same time a biting satire on
unlicensed self-expression.

'Mellonta Tauta,' one of Poe's last satirical pieces (February
1849), develops many of the themes outlined in his pseudo-
scientific essay 'Eureka', and was apparently intended as an
extended critique of American institutions and attitudes in
the 1840s. Dated 1 April, 2848, the story purports to be a letter
(by a writer signing himself 'Pundita') written on board the
balloon 'Skylark' and recounting a voyage by balloon over
America and Canada in the distant future. It is written
throughout in light-hearted style, as befitting a story dated on
April Fool's Day, and Poe uses the opportunity of the
imaginary voyage to satirise his contemporaries whilst enjoying a bird's-eye view of the scene below him.

The title is a quotation from 'Eureka': 'my reply is that
mellonta tauta – I am but pausing, for a moment, on the awful
threshold of *the Future*', and in common with his other
exercises in the genre, 'Mellonta Tauta' abounds in passages
in which Poe, with evident relish, lampoons contemporary
social and political institutions, e.g.: 'I rejoice, my dear friend,
that we live in an age so enlightened that no such a thing as an
individual is supposed to exist. It is the mass for which the true
Humanity cares.' And again, 'Every man "voted", as they
called it – that is to say, meddled with public affairs – until, at
length, it was discovered that what is everybody's business is

nobody's, and that the "Republic" (so the absurd thing was called) was without a government at all.' What emerges very clearly from this story is Poe's evident distaste for democracy (or at least democracy as it was practised in the America of his time) and his profound pessimism concerning the future of his country. He did not foresee a future of progress and enlightenment, as did many facile prophets of the day – influenced by notions of 'human perfectibility' – but forecast instead a nightmare world of overcrowding and conflict in which material advance is at the expense of the human spirit. Indeed the world of 2848 resembles nothing so much as the London of the twenty-first century described by H. G. Wells exactly fifty years later in *When the Sleeper Wakes*. For the world as seen from the balloon 'Skylark' is one in which 'the destruction of a myriad of individuals is only so much positive advantage to the mass,' in which speed has become an end in itself, and in which freedom of thought is subservient to 'Consistency'.

Throughout the narrative Poe is at pains to deflate the seriousness with which contemporary philosophers took themselves and their works. This can be seen in the frequent references to 'a Turkish philosopher (or Hindoo possibly) called Aries Tottle', in the references to an omniscient writer called 'Pundit' whose word on all things is final, and in the numerous quotations from his own work 'Eureka', published in the previous year. He seems to have intended 'Mellonta Tauta' to be regarded as a companion piece to the earlier work, and it is significant that having taken immense pains over the writing of 'Eureka' – for which he received only fourteen dollars from the publisher – he was able to smile at himself in the form of this irreverent spoof.

Beyond this, the final sentence, 'I shall cork the MS. up in a bottle however, and throw it into the sea,' recalls his short story 'MS. Found in a Bottle', the tale with which he began his career as a short story writer. Poe had indeed travelled full circle. Between the hopeful young writer of twenty-four and the tormented and ill writer of forty there lay sixteen years of struggle and disillusionment, years lit by the occasional success but marked for the most part by poverty and tedium. Looking ahead, he could see little hope for his fellow men. Casting about for a suitable form in which to express his fears for mankind, he chose not the terrifying veracity of his earlier tales but the device of a facetious cynical observer looking down on civilisation from above. Even at the end his sense of humour did not desert him.

* * * * *

In August 1846, dissatisfied with the collection of his work published under the title *Tales* (New York, 1845) since in his view this failed to represent the whole range of his talent, Poe wrote to his friend Philip P. Cooke projecting a wider collection of his short stories:

> Were all my Tales now before me in a large volume and as the composition of another – the merit which would princi- pally arrest my attention would be the wide *diversity and variety* . . .. There is a vast variety of kinds and, in degree of value, these kinds vary – but each tale is equally good of its *kind*.

He was unquestionably right to draw attention to the diversity of his literary range. It is fashionable to castigate Poe for the narrowness of his imaginative framework but in fact the range of his work is remarkably wide. In *setting* his stories range widely over England, Europe and America and in *form* he embraced most varieties of the short story with the exception of the anecdote of domestic life. Reviewing his work in its entirety it would be difficult to deny that his influence upon the short story as an art form has been immense. Uneven in quality – and taking into account the circumstances of his private life it is astonishing that he was able to produce so much of outstanding merit – his work is nonetheless remarkable for its haunting quality and its vivid insight into the darker regions of the imagination. In two distinct genres, the horror story and the short tale of detection, he established the rationale of his medium and paved the way for a whole generation of later writers. In other genres – science fiction, satire and allegory, fantasy – his contribution was also very considerable and has exercised an influence upon literature, both English and European, which has been incalculable. When every allowance has been made for his imperfections and for the over-melodramatic quality of some of his gothic narratives, the fact remains that Edgar Allan Poe penned some of the finest short stories in the English language and that he merits an honoured place in literary history for his creative achievement.

Part IV

THE ROMANCES

The Romances

If one defines a romance as 'a work of prose fiction in which the scenes and incidents are more or less removed from common life and are surrounded by a halo of mystery, an atmosphere of strangeness and adventure' (William Rose Benet, *The Reader's Encyclopaedia*) then it readily becomes apparent that Poe's contribution to the genre has been very considerable. Even more pronounced has been the influence of his stories and literary techniques upon later writers, including figures as diverse as Jules Verne, Bulwer Lytton and Conan Doyle: in this context is meant the Conan Doyle of *The Maracot Deep* and 'The Horror of the Heights' rather than of the Sherlock Holmes stories.

Poe was significant in that he was one of the first writers to make use of the burgeoning possibilities of science and to give these possibilities literary expression in the form of fiction. His life coincided with a plethora of scientific and technical developments in which he displayed the keenest interest – the balloon, automata, the electric telegraph, the daguerrotype, the steamship, and so on. Many of these developments he eulogised in his satirical short story 'The Thousand and Second Tale of Scheherazade' and he did not hesitate to introduce in his stories ideas and themes suggested by the world of science. Indeed Edgar Allan Poe may rightly be regarded not only as the 'father' of the detective story but also as the 'father' of science fiction. The term itself seems to have been unknown in his time, but there can be no question that he was one of its very earliest exponents, pre-dating the works of Jules Verne by a generation. His importance as a writer of science fiction and as a potent influence upon the literature of our own times can be seen most clearly in three stories: 'The

Unparalleled Adventure of One Hans Pfaall' (1835), *The Narrative of Arthur Gordon Pym* (1838) and 'The Balloon-Hoax' (1844).

THE UNPARALLELED ADVENTURE OF ONE HANS PFAALL

This is one of Poe's earliest exercises in a genre he was later to make all his own: that of the quasi-scientific hoax presented as an authentic account of actual events. Such tales as 'A Descent into the Maelström' and 'Von Kempelen and his Discovery' are other examples of the genre; each relies for its effects on plausible narration, clever use of supporting detail and convincing deployment of scientific background.

'Hans Pfaall' contains a number of clues designed to warn the unwary reader that the narrative he is about to read is not all that it appears to be. The ascent to the moon takes place on 1 April; the burgomaster of Rotterdam is named as 'Mynheer Superbus Von Underduk'; the astronomers of the world are described as 'to say the least of the matter, not a whit better, nor greater, nor wiser than they ought to be'; even the name of the hero himself, Pfaall, suggests the word 'laugh' inverted. Despite these hints the story seems to have taken many readers unawares, such is Poe's skill as a storyteller.

The story purports to be a factual account of a journey to the moon by balloon, written by a certain Hans Pfaall, a bellows-mender of Rotterdam. After a few pages of preliminary narration – inessential to the story itself but designed to explain how the 'unparalleled adventure' came to fall into the hands of the President of the College of Astronomers – Pfaall launches at once into a spirited and apparently authentic account of his journey through space, one of the most remarkable pieces of writing Poe ever attempted. It was written at a time when, in the aftermath of John Allan's death (March 1834) and the ending of his hopes of a legacy from the will, he was seeking to earn a reputation for himself as a writer of short stories. Encouraged by the reception of 'MS. Found in a Bottle' he had followed this up with 'The Visionary' (now known as 'The Assignation') and with two brilliant horror stories, 'Berenice' and 'Morella'. He now embarked on the longest tale he had yet attempted, a sustained and vividly imagined account of a journey from the earth to the moon, in which he made full use of his exceptional imaginative powers. In a footnote to the story Poe commented that previous attempts to describe lunar voyages had been notable for their absence of *plausibility* in the details of the journey, and complained that the writers appeared to be ignorant of basic astronomical data. In contrast to these earlier romances 'Hans Pfaall' is notable for its apparent authenticity – an effect which is achieved by the continual reiteration of realistic details and by the ingenuity with which the narrator succeeds in extricating himself during his journey from all manner of precarious situations. This combination of realism with a strong narrative line clearly derives in part from Poe's close study of the works of Defoe; to these he now added the further dimension of scientific accuracy. The result is a short story which merits a place in literary history as the precursor of a host of subsequent journeys to the strange worlds of space.

Poe's approach is not simply scientific to the exclusion of everyday details. The story abounds in circumstantial anecdotes such as the incident regarding the cat aboard the balloon: 'Puss, who seemed in a great measure recovered from her illness, now made a hearty meal of the dead bird, and then went to sleep with much apparent satisfaction: Her kittens were quite lively, and so far evinced not the slightest sign of any uneasiness.' It is touches such as this, so matter of fact and homely, which add verisimilitude to the story and strengthen the credulity of the reader. It is a technique which was to be employed on a fuller canvas in *The Narrative of Arthur Gordon Pym* three years later, but already in 'Hans Pfaall' there are clear indications of the storytelling powers which were to earn for Poe a world-wide posthumous renown. This can be seen, for example, in the circumstantial and brilliantly imagined description of the launch from the earth, in the lucid descriptions of the earth *as seen from the outside*, in the sense of excitement communicated to the reader as the balloon approaches nearer and nearer to the moon. The sense of participation, of actually experiencing a voyage through space, is vividly conveyed. The reader shares with Pfaall in experiencing his emotions as he describes his incredible yet grippingly narrated adventures.

The description of the lunar surface is striking in its accuracy:

> The entire absence of ocean or sea, and indeed of any lake or river, or body of water whatsoever, struck me, at the first glance, as the most extraordinary feature in its geological condition. Yet, strange to say, I beheld vast level regions of a character decidedly alluvial, although by far the greater portion of the hemisphere in sight was covered with innumerable volcanic mountains, conical in shape, and having more the appearance of artificial than of natural protuberances.

To the present day reader, hardened by repeated Apollo moon landings, the wildest parts of the story are those describing *live* volcanoes on the surface and even a population of 'ugly little people'. Yet by the standards of his time his imaginary account of the moon is by no means so reprehensible. Just as in *Pym* he sought to give an intelligent visualisation of the polar regions so in 'Hans Pfaall' he essayed an imaginary picture of the lunar surface which is remarkable in its clarity and prescience.

Writing years later in his essay 'The Literati of New York', Poe stated that the inspiration for the story had come from reading Sir John Herschel's *A Treatise on Astronomy*. 'The theme excited my fancy, and I longed to give free rein to it in depicting my day-dreams about the scenery of the moon – in short, I longed to write a story embodying these dreams.' 'Hans Pfaall' should be seen, then, not simply as an ingenious hoax (although Poe would have been highly amused to learn that many readers took it at face value) but as a first sketch of a genre which has exercised an immense influence on twentieth-century science fiction. In giving 'free rein' to his imaginative speculations about the moon Poe was giving fictional form to that scientific curiosity and sense of wonder which engendered the fantasy literature of our own age.

THE NARRATIVE OF ARTHUR GORDON PYM

In February 1836 Poe, via his friend J. K. Paulding of New York, offered his collection of short stories 'The Tales of the Folio Club' to Harper & Brothers the publishers. The collection had been with Carey & Lea of Philadelphia for a considerable time but still remained unpublished. After consideration Harper's also declined to publish the volume, requesting Paulding to say on their behalf:

They desire me, however, to state to Mr. Poe that if he will lower himself a little to the ordinary comprehension of the generality of readers, and prepare a series of original Tales or a single work, and send them to the Publishers, previous to their appearance in the *Messenger*, [the *Southern Literary Messenger*, of which Poe was assistant editor from August 1835–January 1837] they will make such arrangements with him as will be liberal and satisfactory.

Paulding went on to add 'I think it would be worth your while, if other engagements permit, to undertake a Tale in a couple of volumes, for that is the magical number.' Poe took this advice to heart and began work at once on *The Narrative of Arthur Gordon Pym*. This was to be his only full-length novel – discounting the unfinished and far less successful *Journal of Julius Rodman* (1840) which never achieved publication in book form in his lifetime – and the fourth volume of his work to be published.

The phrase 'if he will lower himself a little to the ordinary comprehension of the generality of readers' is significant. What Harper's meant by this, and were probably too polite to say outright, was that they considered Poe's stories to be too other-worldly, too abstruse, for the bulk of their readership and that they required from him a long story dealing not with gruesome horrors and the morbid details of death but with more normal human situations. In the event, as will be seen, his manuscript was an entirely characteristic piece of work which includes in full measure cruelty, violence, savagery and murder and which embraces also many of his most fundamental concerns as a writer.

The first instalment of *Arthur Gordon Pym* appeared in the

Southern Literary Messenger in January 1837 and a second instalment followed in February. Thereafter the serialisation ceased, possibly because Harper's were anxious to copyright the book, which was duly done in June of that year. The evidence suggests that Poe continued to work on the story throughout 1837, writing, revising, and moulding his narrative into a coherent and carefully wrought whole. The magazine instalments were published under Poe's own name, but when the book came out (in July 1838) he was careful to preface the volume with an introduction ostensibly written by 'A. G. Pym' and asserting that, whilst the *Messenger* articles had been written by Poe under the guise of fiction, the whole of the remainder was a factual account written by Pym. It seems most probable, therefore, that on reflection Poe decided to remove his own name from the title page and present the book as an authentic record of actual events, after the manner of *Robinson Crusoe*. Indeed a comparison of the title pages of the two romances reveals at once that Poe was following in the footsteps of a distinguished literary tradition:

The Life and Strange Surprising Adventures of Robinson Crusoe, of York, Mariner: Who lived Eight and Twenty Years, all alone in an uninhabited Island on the Coast of America, near the Mouth of the Great River of Oroonoque; Having been cast on Shore by Shipwreck, wherein all the Men perished but himself. With An Account how he was at last as strangely delivered by Pirates. Written by Himself.

The Narrative of Arthur Gordon Pym of Nantucket; Comprising the Details of a Mutiny and Atrocious Butchery on board the American Brig *Grampus*, on her Way to the South Seas – with an Account of the Recapture of the Vessel by the Survivors; their Shipwreck, and subsequent Horrible Sufferings from Famine; their Deliverance by means of the British Schooner *Jane Guy*; the brief Cruise of this latter Vessel in the Antarctic Ocean, her Capture, and the Massacre of her Crew among a Group of Islands in the 84th Parallel of Southern Latitude; together with the incredible Adventures and Discoveries still further South, to which that distressing Calamity gave rise.

All his life Poe had been fascinated by the sea. He had after all experienced two transatlantic voyages whilst still a young man, and had spent much of his life in and around seaports and imbibing seafaring yarns. He possessed therefore a considerable knowledge of nautical expressions and lore gained largely from personal experience aboard ship. To this he could add a mass of seafaring detail derived from his miscellaneous reading over a period of many years. He had read such books as Morrell's *Narrative of Four Voyages to the South Sea and the Pacific*, J. L. Stephens' *Travels in Arabia Petraea*, Washington Irving's *Astoria*, and J. N. Reynolds' *South Sea Expedition*. He had also re-read *Robinson Crusoe*, one of his favourite boyhood tales, and had been impressed anew with Defoes' craftsmanship as a story-teller and mastery of circumstantial detail. All these ingredients, combined with his own vivid imagination, fused together in the making of *The Narrative of Arthur Gordon Pym*.

The opening chapter, with its restrained manner and interesting autobiographical detail – Poe includes some of the background of his early life in Richmond, including his schooling and boyhood escapades – forms the prelude to the main body of the narrative which must be one of the most exciting stories of adventure and suffering at sea ever written. There can be no question that in the writing of it Poe drew freely upon other literary sources, including *The Rime of the Ancient Mariner*, but it is equally clear that he brought to the task his own exceptional creative gifts and his capacity for the writing of a convincing, taut and gripping story.

What distinguishes the tale as a chronicle of human bravery and suffering is his extremely skilful use of circumstantial detail in building up a narrative which is at once astonishing and verisimilar. The constant reiteration of factual details, the accumulation of names and dates, the appeals to the credulity and understanding of the reader – all these devices lend veracity to the story. Indeed it is hardly surprising that some readers were completely taken in by it and felt it was so convincingly written that it could not possibly be a work of fiction. The following passage is an entirely typical example of Poe's technique:

Augustus still lay senseless in the bottom of the boat; and as there was imminent danger of his drowning (the water being nearly a foot deep just where he fell), I contrived to raise him partially up, and keep him in a sitting position, by passing a rope round his waist, and lashing it to a ringbolt in the deck of the cuddy. Having thus arranged everything as well as I could in my chilled and agitated condition, I recommended myself to God, and made up my mind to bear whatever might happen with all the fortitude in my power.[1]

It is this deft use of circumstantial material, minutely detailed – the reference to the depth of the water in the boat, the 'chilled and agitated condition' of the narrator, the appeal to God, the decision to bear all with fortitude – which lends to the story such a convincing atmosphere of realism. Clearly the style owes much to *Robinson Crusoe* and *A Journal of the Plague Year*. Equally clearly it is a style which has been successfully emulated by many of those who came after Poe: Jules Verne, for example, in such tales as *A Journey to the Centre of the Earth* and Rider Haggard in his African romances. But in 1838 the vivid documentary style of *Pym* was still relatively new; one has only to compare it with such romances as Mary Shelley's *Frankenstein* (1818) and *The Last Man* (1826) to realise how far less 'gothic' and more easily assimilable Poe's manner of narration is by comparison with his European contemporaries.

The greater part of the book – seventeen chapters out of twenty-five – forms an enthralling account of adventure at sea in the course of which Pym witnesses mutiny and murder, almost dies of starvation, and is finally rescued by a British ship, the *Jane Guy*, bound on a voyage to the South Seas. These chapters are so carefully executed and replete with such a body of convincing detail that, though the reader's credulity is strained at one or two points, there is no stage at which belief is altogether suspended. Poe's craftsmanship as a storyteller is such that the reader identifies fully with Pym and shares his emotions, fears and tensions through all his experiences. However the final section of the narrative, in which the *Jane Guy* lands on an island in the Antarctic and thereafter, after a series of incredible adventures, Pym embarks for the polar regions, has been much criticised on the grounds of its inherent implausibility. Black natives in the Antarctic (apparently conversing in Hebrew), an island in the polar seas bearing abundant flora and fauna, mysterious carvings in Arabic – all these were too incredible for many readers and tended to weaken the effectiveness of the book as a whole. These passages are more readily comprehensible, however, when interpreted with a view to their symbolic rather than their literal meaning.

Pym is so outraged at the duplicity and savagery of the islanders (they pretend to befriend the party of white explorers whilst in reality scheming their massacre) that he condemns them as 'among the most barbarous, subtle and bloodthirsty wretches that ever contaminated the face of the globe'.[2] Critics have seen in this and similar passages evidence that Poe was deliberately playing on Southern hysteria by suggesting that negroes were in reality a treacherous and hostile people; seen in these terms the concluding chapters are said to be an elaborate allegory on racial inequality and intolerance. My own reading does not support this view, but would argue as an alternative interpretation that the islanders symbolise the Mob, the Many, the unthinking majority which Poe so evidently feared and despised. Again and again in his work he expressed his animus towards the Mob. (Cf. 'Some Words with a Mummy', in which the Mob is described as 'the usurping tyrant' and the United States as 'the most odious and insupportable despotism that was ever heard of upon the face of the Earth'.) Viewed in this context the black and sinister islanders of Tsalal represent all those forces which stand for the antithesis of the unfettered imagination: intolerance, prejudice, fear and hypocrisy.

This becomes clearer in the final chapter, in which the hero is drawn irresistibly towards the South Pole and (in a passage strongly reminiscent of the ending of 'MS. Found in a Bottle') Pym describes with mounting suspense the relentless journey towards his unknown fate. It has to be remembered that the South Pole was not discovered by man until the year 1911. At the time when Poe was writing the fashionable theory, known as 'Symmes's hole', was that the earth was hollow and open at the two poles: that at each pole the sea plunged into the earth in a whirlpool of terrifying depth. The polar regions clearly exercised a strong fascination for Poe and in describing the voyage of his hero towards the ultimate maelström he is giving fictional expression to some of his most vivid imaginings.[3] (During his final delirium it is recorded that Poe repeatedly called out in his death-agony 'Reynolds! Reynolds! Oh, Reynolds!' Jeremiah N. Reynolds was the author of a pamphlet publicising the 'Symmes's hole' theory of the poles and urging the case for an expedition to verify it. Did Poe, on his death-bed, feel himself being drawn into the vortex he had imagined with such intensity years before?) The story rises to a climax of unforgettable tension and grandeur as the boat rushes towards the vortex:

> And now we rushed into the embraces of the cataract, where a chasm threw itself open to receive us. But there arose in our pathway a shrouded human figure, very far larger in its proportions than any dweller among men. And the hue of the skin of the figure was of the perfect whiteness of the snow.

This enigmatic ending, so characteristic of Poe, perfectly knits together both the realistic and allegorical elements which are interwoven throughout the story. Pym, unlike the narrator of 'MS. Found in a Bottle', survives to tell the tale: this is implicit in the publication of his narrative. The 'shrouded human figure' then, we must assume, is in some way the agent of his escape from the awesome cataract. Symbolically also the ending represents release: the escape of the imagination from an alien world; the release of the human spirit from imprisonment and death. Throughout the narrative Pym has sought to escape from one restricting situation after another – from the coffin-like box in which he is confined as a stowaway, from the hold of the ship, from starvation and death aboard the *Grampus*, from the avalanche of rocks precipitated by the islanders, from the island itself, and lastly from the vortex of the pole. It is not difficult to see in this continual pattern of confinement and release an extended parable on a theme which lay at the centre of Poe's concerns thoughout his adult life: that of the overriding importance of the human imagination, its refusal to be compromised by the lowering of critical standards, and its antipathy towards those elements which sought to fetter it. What begins then, as an exciting adventure story in the vein of Defoe becomes, in Poe's hands, a profoundly serious allegory on the release of the imagination from oblivion. The whole work is indeed both an actual and a spiritual journey: the journey of Arthur Gordon Pym towards self-fulfilment and, in a deeper sense, the journey of the imaginative artist towards the utmost freedom of expression.

*   *   *   *   *

Although the book was widely reviewed in the United States[4] and received some attention in England (where, as with 'Valdemar', it was assumed to be a factual account) it was not a commercial success and Poe received very little money from it. It is difficult to understand the reasons for this, since Harper's was then, as now, one of the major American publishing houses and Poe in 1838 was by no means an unknown writer. In retrospect it may be that the readers of the time found the tale too morbid, that the continual accumulation of harrowing detail was simply too much to accept and was felt to exceed the bounds of good taste. (In one scene, for example, a leg drops off a gangrenous body while it is being thrown into the sea; in another scene two starving men kill and eat a third). Or it may be that the complex interplay of symbolism and allegory which Poe seems to have intended was not fully comprehended, and the story was seen as a catalogue of far-fetched horrors and little more. Whatever the explanation, the fact remains that sales of *Pym* were discouraging and Poe must have felt that he had little to show for his year's work. The significance of the book to the student of literature is twofold: first, in its effect upon Poe himself as a writer and, second, in its impact on subsequent writers as a source of inspiration and ideas. In both these areas its importance was far-reaching.

Pym is not a novel of character in the accepted sense – it is rather an exciting tale of adventure in the vein of Marryat or Fenimore Cooper – yet the character and personality of the central figure, Arthur Gordon Pym, unquestionably develops as the story proceeds. At the outset of the book he is an immature, rather foolish young man, lacking in self-confidence and with little knowledge of the world outside his native town. In the course of the narrative his adventures and experiences are such that he emerges from them not only considerably wiser but with greatly enhanced courage and self-reliance. He has witnessed deception, cruelty, savagery and violence; he has seen bravery, suffering, loyalty and compassion; he has been tried and tested. Pym in fact witnesses the whole gamut of human emotions and weaknesses and as a consequence of all he has undergone he gains maturity. Whether Poe identified himself wholly with his hero is debatable, but certainly the author gained a perspective and a sense of detachment from the writing of *Pym* which is evident in all his subsequent work. During the ten years of his life that remained to him after the publication of his one novel Poe produced his very finest work, including 'The Fall of the House of Usher', 'The Murders in the Rue Morgue', 'The Pit and the Pendulum', 'The Tell-Tale Heart' and 'The Gold-Bug': tales which are known and respected throughout the world. In the travail of writing *Pym* he had progressed from a tyro to an accomplished and assured writer of proven narrative skill; the book was in a real sense an apprenticeship, in the course of which he learned the craft of the storyteller.

Much has been written concerning the possible influence of Poe's romance on Melville's *Moby Dick* (1851),[5] and certainly Melville seems to have borrowed a number of incidents and ideas from Poe, but the book has exercised an even more marked effect on twentieth-century literature. It is interesting, for example, to trace the influence of *The Narrative of Arthur Gordon Pym* on later writers, most notably upon H. G. Wells. Bernard Bergonzi has pointed out that some of the incidents in *The Island of Doctor Moreau* – including the drawing of lots to decide which of the survivors shall be eaten, and the idea of a boat containing a crew of dead men – may well be derived from *Pym*. That Wells had read and admired *Pym* there can be no doubt, for it is referred to explicitly in his autobiography.[6] But it is upon his satirical and allegorical story *Mr. Blettsworthy on Rampole Island* (1928) that Poe's romance exercised the most profound influence. Compare, firstly, the title page of *Pym* (page 120) with that of Wells's narrative:

Being the Story of a Gentleman of Culture and Refinement who suffered Shipwreck and saw no Human Beings other than Cruel and Savage Cannibals for several years. How he beheld Megatheria alive and made some notes of their Habits. How he became a Sacred Lunatic. How he did at last escape in a Strange Manner from the Horror and Barbarities of Rampole Island in time to fight in the Great War, and how afterwards he came near returning to that Island for ever. With much Amusing and Edifying Matter concerning Manners, Customs, Beliefs, Warfare, Crime, and a Storm at Sea. Concluding with some Reflections upon Life in General and upon these Present Times in Particular.

Here Wells is consciously employing the literary devices employed by Poe to arouse the curiosity and interest of the reader. In both instances there is a preview of the extraordinary events about to be unfolded (Poe: mutiny, butchery, shipwreck, sufferings, deliverance, capture, massacre; Wells: shipwreck, cannibals, escape, barbarities, war, crime, storm at sea). There is the same emulation of the circumstantial title page favoured by such precursors as Defoe, and the same desire to present the narrative as an authentic record set down by a lone survivor. Both title-pages also conclude with a promise clearly aimed at whetting the readers' appetite further:

together with the incredible Adventures and Discoveries still further South, to which that distressing Calamity gave rise.

Pym

With much Amusing and Edifying Matter concerning Manners, Customs, Beliefs, Warfare, Crime, and a Storm at Sea.

Blettsworthy

There are a number of similarities between the two narratives, both in style and content. In both there is a long sea voyage, a mutiny, and a storm which incapacitates the ship. In both there is a murder aboard ship and burial at sea. In both there is a circumstantial description of an island inhabited by savages and a detailed account of their customs and way of life. (It is interesting to note that in both accounts of the island a gorge or ravine plays a significant role: in *Pym* as the scene of the avalanche in which most of the crew lose their lives, and in *Blettsworthy* as the cleft in which the hero hides from his pursuers and from which he ultimately returns to civilisation.[7]) At one point in his narrative Poe mentions an incident in which a shark actually comes aboard the ship:

> Towards evening saw several sharks, and were somewhat alarmed by the audacious manner in which an enormously large one approached us. At one time, a lurch throwing the deck very far beneath the water, the monster actually swam in upon us, floundering for some moments just over the companion hatch, and striking Peters violently with his tail. A heavy sea at length hurled him overboard, much to our relief.

Wells introduces an identical episode in his narrative:

> And I saw one thing no one will believe. I saw a great shark come aboard. A wave, tall and pointed like the Jungfrau, towered up over the side. . . . and there, rolling across the deck leeward, bending itself into a bow and flashing out straight again and snapping like an angry square-mouthed handbag, was this great white-bellied fish. It was enormously bigger than a man. It lashed and flung itself about, trailing threads of slime after it that blew straight out in the wind. It was bloody under its belly. The ship seemed for a moment to survey our new shipmate with amazement, and then with a resolute effort rolled it and the swirling foam it came with, over the starboard rail as though there were some things that even a disabled ocean tramp would not endure.[8]

This is an interesting example of the manner in which subsequent writers have taken an idea by Poe, developed it, and then incorporated it within their own material. In this instance the *initial idea* clearly originates with Poe but it has been expanded by the addition of much circumstantial detail, giving a further element of verisimilitude to the account. It is precisely in this regard – as a source of ideas and concepts in fiction – that Poe has exercised such a seminal influence on twentieth-century literature.

Writing to Julian Huxley during the composition of *Mr. Blettsworthy on Rampole Island* Wells referred to it as 'my fantastic pseudo boys' adventure story which will be my *Candide*, my *Peer Gynt*, my *Gulliver'*.[9] He might have added *Arthur Gordon Pym* as one of the exemplars which clearly influenced his work and which provided some of the basic sources he drew upon in constructing his own satirical tale.

THE BALLOON-HOAX

On 13 April 1844 the offices of the *New York Sun* were besieged with excited crowds clamouring for copies of the broadside (a special issue printed on one side only) which had been promised for 10 a.m. It was not until almost twelve noon, however, that the 'Extra' appeared, and such was the demand for copies that Poe himself, the cause of the excitement, was unable to buy one.

The *Sun* was a cheap newspaper which made a speciality of the sensational presentation of news. Nine years earlier the editor, Richard Adams Locke, had hoaxed his readers with a spurious story – inspired by Poe's 'Hans Pfaall' – describing a telescope which had revealed life on the moon. Now he was hoaxing the public again with a manuscript he had purchased from Poe purporting to describe the world's first Atlantic crossing by balloon. The headlines were certainly sensational enough:

ASTOUNDING
NEWS!
BY EXPRESS VIA NORFOLK!
THE
ATLANTIC CROSSED
in
THREE DAYS!

———

Signal Triumph
of
Mr. Monck Mason's
FLYING
MACHINE!!!!

Arrival at Sullivan's Island near Charleston, S. C. of Mr.
Mason, Mr. Robert Holland, Mr. Henson, Mr. Harrison
Ainsworth, and four others, in the Steering Balloon
'Victoria'—After a passage of Seventy-Five Hours From
Land to Land! Full Particulars of the Voyage!

The entire narrative reveals Poe's gift for creating verisimilitude by the skilful use of circumstantial detail. He had
always been interested in hoaxes (his most celebrated fabri-
cated tale, 'The Facts in the Case of M. Valdemar', was to follow
in December 1845) and in 'The Balloon-Hoax' he set out to
make his story as convincing and minutely detailed as possible.
The use of the names of actual people, e.g., Monck Mason and
Harrison Ainsworth, and of real places, e.g., Sullivan's Island
(which Poe knew well from his days as an Army private and
had previously used as the setting for his ingenious short
story 'The Gold-Bug') inevitably lent a convincing air of
authenticity to his narrative. Monck Mason was the inventor
of a mechanically driven dirigible balloon which had been
exhibited in London in 1843; Harrison Ainsworth was a
well-known historical novelist whose work Poe had reviewed
and whose style he now sought to parody. The device of
employing actual names and dates is one which fifty years later
Wells was to adopt with brilliant effect in *The War of the Worlds*.
Indeed the closest parallel in our own times to the sensation
caused by the publication of 'The Balloon-Hoax' is that
surrounding Orson Welles's dramatised version of *The War of
the Worlds* (as a Halloween jape) in 1938.

It is perhaps difficult for readers today to understand the
intense excitement and interest with which 'The Balloon-
Hoax' was received on its original publication. The newspapers had speculated about the possibilities of Atlantic flight
for some years: in 1840 an Englishman, a certain Charles
Green, had actually built a model of an Atlantic Balloon which
had successfully flown. Poe, discussing the matter in *Burton's
Gentleman's Magazine*, had commented 'For our own part, so
far from gainsaying one word that the aeronaut asserts, we
have for a long time past wondered why it was that our own
Wise [John Wise, an American balloonist] had not aeronauted
himself over to Europe – than which nothing could be a more
feasible manoeuvre'. The special issue of the *Sun* containing

Poe's spurious but extremely plausible-sounding and circumstantial account must then have burst upon an astonished New York with all the impact of the first moon landings in 1969.

Poe achieves his effects with a range of literary devices, at each of which he was adept. The detailed and matter of fact description of the balloon and its launching, the convincing air of scientific knowledge, the continually reiterated factual minutiæ – all combine to create an impression of veracity. Poe goes beyond these techniques by deliberately casting his account in the form of a journal, ostensibly written by Mr. Mason but with postscripts added by Harrison Ainsworth. This device permits the reader to see the events described from different points of view and is handled with extreme deftness, even to the extent of imitating Ainsworth's rather florid style of narration. The result is to add a perspective and immediacy to the story it would otherwise have lacked and to heighten the narrative (e.g., Ainsworth's comment 'The last nine hours have been unquestionably the most exciting of my life. I can conceive nothing more sublimating than the strange peril and novelty of an adventure such as this') with a sense of tension which is vividly communicated to the reader.

Now that the transatlantic balloon crossing has been achieved – the first successful flight occurred a century after Poe's extraordinarily prescient account – something of the wonder and excitement of the story has inevitably been lost. For the perceptive reader, however, this strengthens rather than diminishes his achievement. In the creation of stories such as 'The Balloon-Hoax' and 'Hans Pfaall' he was laying the foundations of an entire genre of twentieth-century science fiction and anticipating much of the methodology of the literature of space travel. He was widening the frontiers of the short story to embrace a new kind of fictional narrative, *the tale of scientific anticipation*, which, in the hands of such practitioners as Verne and Wells, has proved such a fruitful source of imaginative achievement. In doing so he was fusing together the narrative skill he had perfected during a long apprenticeship as a writer of grotesque stories with the scientific curiosity we normally associate with our own century.

* * * * *

Poe's influence on both Anglo-American and European

science fiction has been profound. Indeed he can in a real sense be regarded as 'the father of science fiction' since later writers, from Verne onwards, demonstrably owe so much to his pioneering vision. His stories have been influential not only in that he foreshadowed many technological developments which did not become a reality until our own time but also in the sense that he was one of the first writers to fuse the rational with the symbolical in a coherent imaginative whole. His 'science fiction' stories are never simply *stories*: they are rich in allegorical and satirical undertones which add a dimension of symbolism to the surface account. This blending of storytelling and didacticism has been immensely influential and can be traced, for example, through Wells and Orwell to Robert Heinlein, James Blish and Damon Knight. Moreover, in seeking to assess Poe's seminal contribution to the literature of our own century we should not lose sight of his underlying seriousness of purpose. The fact that he chose to present some of his scientific speculations in the guise of satires or hoaxes could lead to the assumption that he approached his work in a light-hearted manner: nothing could be further from the truth. He was above all things an intensely serious literary artist, striving consciously to make his mark on posterity, and this is nowhere more evident than in his scientific romances. With his numerous explanatory footnotes, his references to distinguished scientists and philosophers and his frequent quotations from learned works he brought something of the apparatus of scholarship to his tales and could be described as the first *theoretician* of science fiction. This deliberate attempt to cast sensational stories in a literary form and to give them a rationale has exercised a most potent influence on English letters and is one which is even yet bearing fruit in the myths of our age. His tragedy was to have been born a hundred years ahead of his time and to have lived in an intellectual climate when his unusual gifts were virtually unrecognised until long after his death.

Jules Verne, writing in 1864, observed of him: 'You might call him "The Leader of the Cult of the Unusual"; he has thrust back the bounds of what is impossible. He will certainly have imitators: those who seek to go beyond him, to exaggerate his style; but plenty of those who fancy that they have surpassed him, and will not even have equalled him.'

Part V

ESSAYS AND CRITICISM

Essays and Criticism

During Poe's lifetime James Russell Lowell said of him:

> Mr. Poe is at once the most discriminating, philosophical,
> and fearless critic upon imaginative works who has written
> in America.... If we do not always agree with him in his
> premises, we are, at least, satisfied that his deductions are
> logical, and that we are reading the thoughts of a man who
> thinks for himself, and says what he thinks, and knows well
> what he is talking about. His analytic power would furnish
> bravely forth some score of ordinary critics.

In any assessment of Poe as a critic and essayist it has to be
borne in mind that he was throughout almost all his working
life chronically short of money, and that for this reason he
tended to devote his critical talents to the reviewing of works
by ephemeral authors and poets. (Who today, for example, is
familiar with the writings of Amelia B. Welby or J. G. C.
Brainard?) For the same reason he produced only a small
amount of original writing on critical theory. This is, however,
extremely significant and merits careful attention from all
who seek to understand Poe as man and writer. His most
important contributions to the theory of literary criticism are
the preface to the 1831 edition of the *Poems* ('Letter to
B———'), his review of Hawthorne's *Twice-Told Tales* (1842),
the essay 'The Philosophy of Composition' (1846), and his
final lecture, 'The Poetic Principle' (1849). These will now be
discussed in turn.

*   *   *   *   *

'Letter to B———' [an open letter addressed to Elam Bliss, his
publisher] marks an important landmark in Poe's works in
that it was written almost at the beginning of his career as
journalist and poet. It is a remarkable piece of work for an
unknown writer of twenty-two, clearly owing much to
Coleridge and displaying signs of youthful exuberance, but
containing indications of the mature artist. Beneath its
rambling manner can be discerned the earliest statement of
his theory of poetic criticism. Poe begins the preface with the
observation that it is extremely difficult for an American
writer to be taken seriously, that in the literary world English
and French writers are read with respect and attention but
American authors, particularly if not widely known, hardly at
all, ' . . . . for it is with literature as with law or empire – an
established name is an estate in tenure, or a throne in
possession'. The preface then continues with a criticism of
didactic poetry, arguing strongly against 'the subtleties which
would make poetry a study – not a passion' and singling out
Wordsworth for particular criticism as a metaphysician. Poe
then enlarges on his reverence for Coleridge, praising his
intellectual and creative powers, and concluding with a
concise definition of a poem as he sees it:

> A poem, in my opinion, is opposed to a work of science by
> having, for its *immediate* object, pleasure, not truth: to
> romance, by having for its object an *indefinite* instead of a
> *definite* pleasure, being a poem only so far as this object is
> attained: romance presenting perceptible images with
> definite, poetry with *in*definite sensations, to which end
> music is an essential, since the comprehension of sweet
> sound is our most indefinite conception.

This definition (which Poe copied almost verbatim from
Coleridge's *Biographia Literaria*) remained with him throughout his life and, although these criteria were refined and
elaborated in numerous articles and reviews, he did not in
essence depart from them in the whole of his career as poet,
editor and critic. That the object of a poem was to give
aesthetic pleasure, that it was concerned with indefinite
images, that it was at its most sublime when it achieved
beautiful, musical sounds – these were the principles by which

he measured his own work and which provided the inspiration for his creative achievements. These, moreover, were the criteria which guided his judgments and actions in all he subsequently undertook.

As a book reviewer Poe was compelled by circumstances to devote much of his energies to appraising volumes of indifferent poetry written by obscure authors. By no means all of his reviews fall into this category, however, and many of them are notable for their perceptivity. His review of Augustus Baldwin Longstreet's *Georgia Scenes*, for example, (*Southern Literary Messenger* March 1836) is noteworthy for his prescience in recognising the literary merit of the work which, although published anonymously, can now be seen as a forerunner of the vernacular humour of Mark Twain. Significant also is the famous 'Drake-Halleck review' – a review of *The Culprit Fay and Other Poems* by Joseph Rodman Drake and *Alnwick Castle with Other Poems* by Fitz Greene Halleck (*Southern Literary Messenger* April 1836) – which contains Poe's first major critique of literary provincialism. Of particular interest to English readers are his reviews of Dickens's *Sketches by Boz* – published in the United States under the title *Watkins Tottle* – and *Barnaby Rudge*, both of which reveal a lively appreciation of Dickens's art. It is interesting to note that as early as 1836 Poe described Dickens as 'a far more pungent, more witty and better disciplined writer of sly articles than nine-tenths of the magazine writers in Great Britain'. He added characteristically: 'We cannot bring ourselves to believe that less actual ability is required in the composition of a really good 'brief article', than in a fashionable novel of the usual dimensions.'

Perhaps of most significance as a statement of Poe's own literary theories is his review of Nathaniel Hawthorne's *Twice-Told Tales*, published in *Graham's Magazine* in May 1842. This is important not only as an early appreciation of Hawthorne's stature as a storyteller but as a summary of Poe's intellectual and artistic approach to the art of the short story.

After summarising contemporary critical attitudes to Hawthorne he continues:

There has long existed in literature a fatal and unfounded prejudice, which it will be the office of this age to overthrow – the idea that the mere bulk of a work must enter largely into our estimate of its merit . . . . The tale proper affords the fairest field which can be afforded by the wide domains of mere prose, for the exercise of the highest genius.

The review concludes with a concise summary of his view of literature: that the short poem was the noblest form of artistic expression; that, after poetry, the 'brief prose tale' afforded the finest opportunities for such expression; that the novel, by its very nature, was not a suitable medium for the effect of *totality*; that a short story must aim to achieve a *single effect* which remains in the mind of the reader. 'In the whole composition there should be no word written of which the tendency, direct or indirect, is not the one pre-established design. And by such means, with such care and skill, a picture is at length painted which leaves in the mind of him who contemplates it with a kindred art, a sense of the fullest satisfaction. The idea of the tale, its thesis, has been presented unblemished, because undisturbed – an end absolutely demanded, yet, in the novel, altogether unattainable.'

There is some substance in the observation that in making these claims for the short story as against the novel Poe is simply rationalising from his own experience. For much of his working life he led a hand to mouth existence (the term 'hand to mouth' is literally accurate in his case, since he frequently lacked sufficient money to purchase food, warmth and clothing for himself and his household) and he was obliged by his circumstances to write short pieces at frequent intervals simply in order to survive. In arguing that the short story was artistically and philosophically superior to the full-length prose composition he was to some extent therefore making a virtue of a necessity. Yet he was unquestionably sincere in advancing these claims and it is impossible to understand Poe and his place in literary history without acknowledging the central importance of the theoretical principles which guided him in all he undertook.

Consider, for example, the principles of construction set forth in the same review:

A skilful artist has constructed a tale. He has not fashioned his thoughts to accommodate his incidents, but having deliberately conceived a certain *single effect* to be wrought, he then invents such incidents, he then combines such events, and discusses them in such tone as may best serve him in establishing this preconceived effect. *If his very first sentence tend not to the outbringing of this effect, then in his very first step has he committed a blunder.* [My italics]

How consummately Poe applied these criteria to his own work may be judged from the artistry of such tales as 'The Fall of the House of Usher', 'The Black Cat', 'The Oval Portrait' and 'The Cask of Amontillado'. In the finest of the tales and poems he sought consciously to achieve a single overriding impression – an impression, moreover, which he wished to be *felt* emotionally not merely experienced intellectually. Much of the power of the short stories lies precisely in the extraordinary vividness of their central idea: the intensity of the dominant impression – the descent of the scythe in 'The Pit and the Pendulum', the entry of the supposed corpse in 'The Fall of the House of Usher' and 'Ligeia', the terrible heartbeat in 'The Tell-Tale Heart', the discovery of the walled-up body in 'The Black Cat' – is such as to suspend disbelief and to remain in the imagination of the reader long after the tale has been read. There can also be little doubt that these criteria have in turn influenced many later practitioners of the short story, including Wells, Kipling, Conrad and Stevenson. Indeed Wells as a short story writer has been described as 'the product of a union between Dickens and Poe',[1] and it is interesting to note that at the outset of his literary career Wells was encouraged by the editor of the *Pall Mall Gazette* to write a series of 'single sitting stories': a phrase which Poe would have warmly endorsed. One of Poe's strongest objections to the novel was that it could not be read at one sitting and that mundane distractions, intervening during the pauses between reading, would inevitably diminish the impact of the whole. In the short story, by contrast, the author was able 'to carry out his full design without interruption'.[2]

In his essay 'The Works of Edgar Allan Poe'[3] Stevenson vigorously defended Poe against the charge of pointlessness and asserted:

Pointlessness is, indeed, the very last charge that could be brought reasonably against them [the short stories]. He has the true story-teller's instinct. He knows the little nothings that make stories or mar them. He knows how to enhance the significance of any situation, and give colour and life to seeming irrelevant particulars.

Stevenson, a storyteller of no mean ability himself, is drawing attention in this passage to an extremely interesting aspect of Poe's art – his ability to 'give colour and life to seeming irrelevant particulars' – but Poe would have argued that this was part of a consciously achieved design, that the apparently unimportant details in his tales were deliberately introduced in order to minister to his single overall objective. The melancholy countryside in 'The Fall of the House of Usher', the scholastic background in 'William Wilson', the unidentified beetle in 'The Gold-Bug', the carnival setting of 'The Cask of Amontillado' – all have an important contributory role in achieving the effect or atmosphere he desires, and are in this sense fully consistent with his critical philosophy.

The celebrated essay 'The Philosophy of Composition' is an ingenious attempt to demonstrate how his poem 'The Raven' came to be written. It should not, however, be taken too seriously as an explanation of an actual process of composition but should rather be viewed in the same light as his other exercises in the field of ratiocination, including 'The Gold-Bug' and 'The Murders in the Rue Morgue'. Indeed the essay is principally of interest as a case study in the application of the principles of critical analysis to the process of artistic creation. It has been said of Poe that 'He might have been a great mathematician had his interest been in pure number. He certainly would have made a great detective'.[4] Certainly 'The Philosophy of Composition' contains impressive evidence of his powers as a reasoner and analyst. It is in essence an *ex post facto* study in the logical thought processes which led, step by step, to the composition of 'The Raven', but it is difficult to resist the conclusion that the creation of the poem was in fact a much more lengthy and less scientific process than the essay would suggest. ('The Raven' seems to have been composed over a period of at least four years).[5] Just as, in 'The Murders in the Rue Morgue' and 'The Mystery of Marie Rogêt', he reconstructs the crimes *after* they have taken place, in 'The

Philosophy of Composition' he is reconstructing and rationalising *to himself* a creative process which must, one feels, have been in reality less susceptible to rational analysis. This is not to diminish in any way the validity of the essay as a critical exercise, but merely to assert that it should be regarded as the writer's attempt to explain to his own satisfaction the rationale of the creative process.

In 'The Poetic Principle', the lecture which he prepared in the last year of his life, he presented a concise summary of the critical principles which had guided his work over a period of twenty years. 'A poem', he wrote, 'deserves its title only inasmuch as it excites, by elevating the soul. The value of the poem is in the ratio of this elevating excitement.' The sole purpose of poetry was to minister to man's sense of the beautiful: it had no other purpose beyond this, and to seek to justify poetry on any other grounds was sophistry. Summing up, he encapsulated his philosophy in these terms:

> I would define, in brief, the Poetry of words as *The Rhythmical Creation of Beauty*. Its sole arbiter is Taste. With the Intellect or with the Conscience, it has only collateral relations. Unless incidentally, it has no concern whatever either with Duty or with Truth.

This plea that the sole justification of poetry was the creation of beautiful sounds, that 'in the union of Poetry with Music in its popular sense, we shall find the widest field for the Poetic development', was unquestionably of immense importance to him and provided a critical frame of reference, a rationale against which he measured his own work and that of his contemporaries. The poets he admired most were Coleridge and Shelley; those he admired least were Wordsworth and Longfellow.

Whatever may be the ultimate judgment of Poe's critical principles – and there is some substance in the view that in 'The Poetic Principle' he is once again open to the charge of rationalisation, seeking to provide a theoretical justification for the kind of poetry he himself wrote – there is no gainsaying the seriousness with which he advanced his views or the energy he devoted to the task of disseminating them. During 1848 and 1849, although mentally and physically ill, he lectured on 'The Poetic Principle' on numerous occasions and continued to revise and improve the text (it was published posthumously in 1850). It was as if he sensed that the lecture, together with the philosophical prose poem 'Eureka', would come to be regarded as his final testament. In some of his views – for instance, the argument that a *long* poem could not exist, since this was a contradiction in terms – he was merely being disingenuous, but taken in its entirety his final statement has earned for him widespread critical acclaim. It is an eloquent, even moving, appeal for the importance of poetry to human life, to the role of poetry as evidence of 'the human aspiration for supernal beauty' and as a medium for man's utmost creative endeavours.

*   *   *   *   *

As an essayist Poe wrote entertainingly and lucidly on many diverse subjects over a long period of time. His themes range from a description of his ideal room ('The Philosophy of Furniture') to a study of cryptography ('A Few Words on Secret Writing'), from 'The American Drama' to 'The Business Man'. Among these essays the most interesting and valuable are those in which he gave his imaginative and literary abilities free rein and which allowed him to exercise his unusual gifts of observation and analysis. From this standpoint three representative examples of his technique are 'Diddling', 'The Domain of Arnheim' and 'Eureka'. These will serve to illustrate the diversity of his range and the extraordinary versatility of style and subject-matter at his command.

'Diddling Considered as One of the Exact Sciences' is an interesting example of the light humorous essay which Mark Twain was later to make his own. Beginning with a summary of the characteristic attributes of diddlers, ranging from ingenuity to impertinence, the article then proceeds to a detailed and witty account of nineteenth-century swindles. It should be noted that the tone throughout is one of sympathy for the swindler, not, as one would expect, for the innocent victims of the various sharp practices described. The verbs used to described the diddles are revealing: 'respectable', 'simple', 'bold', 'neat', 'minute', 'scientific' and 'clever'. There is no doubt that hoaxes appealed to some deep-rooted aspect of his sense of humour. This may be seen, for example, in such elaborate deceptions as 'The Balloon-Hoax' and 'Hans Pfaall', and his evident satisfaction at having pulled the wool over the eyes of newspaper editors and readers. There is no mistaking the gusto with which Poe describes the deceptions practised by cheats and diddlers nor the laughter he derives from their activities, a laughter he clearly expects his readers to share. 'Diddling' is important not only because, in the words of Hervey Allen,[6] it throws 'a sidelight on a curious ramification of the man's character', but, more important, because it affords an interesting and extended example of Poe as a humorist. His deserved reputation as a writer of horror stories has served to diminish the other aspects of his art, not least his very real sense of humour. 'Diddling' will repay careful study by any reader who seeks to gain a deeper understanding of Poe as a man of humour and as a literary craftsman thoroughly acquainted with his medium. It is neatly constructed, written with considerable zest, rich in acute observation (e.g., 'Man is an animal that diddles, and there is *no* animal that diddles *but* man') and, above all, it makes no pretence to be anything other than what it is: a facetious commentary upon human fallibilities. In itself it is a refutation of the widely held view that Poe was nothing more than a purveyor of tales of gothic terror.

'The Domain of Arnheim' is one of the most intriguing works ever to come from his pen. Since it is cast in narrative form it has the appearance of a short story and is frequently reprinted as such; in reality, however, it is an extended essay on a theme which was never far from the surface of his imagination – the quest for beauty in an artificially created landscape.

In writing 'The Domain of Arnheim' (and also its 'pendant' or companion piece, 'Landor's Cottage') Poe drew on his childhood memories of a beautiful landscaped garden which stood across from the home of Charles Ellis, John Allan's business partner, in Richmond. As a boy on his way to or from school, and frequently in his childhood games, he must have spent many hours wandering in this quiet place and dreaming among its carefully tended roses, jasmine and honeysuckle. Here in this enchanted garden he indulged in solitary reverie and here, too, he brought his boyhood sweetheart Sarah

Elmira Royster. The place clearly exercised a powerful influence on his imagination and, long after he had left the district, the garden and its associated memories continued to haunt him. It came to symbolise for him a world of peace, of mystical delight, a refuge in which one could find solace and renewal freed from the daily cares and pressures of life. Time and again in his works – in 'the Valley of the Many-Coloured Grass' in his short story 'Eleonora', in 'The Island of the Fay', in the haunting descriptions of natural scenery in 'The Gold-Bug', and in much of the poetry – we find this fascination with the idea of a retreat, an enclosed world cut off from worldly considerations. As he grew older he returned to the idea with inappeasable longing. Blended with these youthful impressions of the garden in Richmond, Poe added his memories of a remote farm he had occupied as a retreat during the summer of 1844 (the farm stood on the Bloomingale Road, five or six miles out of New York) and also of the river scenery near Fordham. 'Arnheim' is then a compound of some of his earliest Richmond memories and the romanticised longings of his last years. The result is an immaculate piece of writing, at once passionate and restrained, in which he gave expression to some of his innermost emotional desires.

Ellison, the central character, is an idealised version of Poe himself, a representation of himself as he would have liked to be:

> In the widest and noblest sense he was a poet. He comprehended, moreover, the true character, the august aims, the supreme majesty and dignity of the poetic sentiment. The fullest, if not the sole proper satisfaction of this sentiment he instinctively felt to lie in the creation of novel forms of beauty.

Ellison inherits a vast fortune and resolves 'that the creation of a landscape-garden offered to the proper Muse the most magnificent of opportunities'. He devotes his wealth to the creation of a man-made paradise, a domain in which he gives full rein to his imaginative and artistic gifts in the taming of nature and the forming of a totally harmonious environment. The domain can only be approached by river, so that its breathtakingly beautiful effects gradually unfold before the visitor. Enchanted by beautiful vistas on each stage of the journey, the visitor emerges at last into a vast amphitheatre in which, apparently suspended in mid-air, is 'a mass of semi-Gothic, semi-Saracenic architecture', the elusive Domain of Arnheim.

To a reader with any understanding of the circumstances of Poe's life this haunting essay can only be found utterly characteristic of the man. In this vision of a sensitive artist dominated by 'that one master passion of his soul, the thirst for beauty', he is clearly giving imaginative expression to his own secret longings. Most revealing of all – and ironic, in the light of his own tragic experiences – is Ellison's yearning for 'the sympathy of a woman, not unwomanly, whose loveliness and love enveloped his existence in the purple atmosphere of Paradise. . . .' In this paradise, this lost domain, Ellison sought to find, and found, *'exemption from the ordinary cases of humanity* [my italics] with a far greater amount of positive happiness than ever glowed in the rapt day-dreams of De Staël'. This conception of a secret, artificially created domain, a remote paradise uncontaminated by ugliness and ignorance, re-mained with him throughout his life and has exercised a profound influence on our literature.[7] With rare exceptions it eluded him yet it never ceased to stimulate his imagination or to inspire some of his most deeply felt writings. It became for him a vision to which he tethered his most intense romantic longings.

Poe unquestionably regarded 'Eureka', written during the tormented months following the death of his wife Virginia, as the culmination of his life's work. To his devoted mother-in-law Maria Clemm he wrote (7 July 1849): 'I have no desire to live since I have done 'Eureka'. I could accomplish nothing more.'

Despite the importance he attached to it – he believed he had 'solved the secret of the universe' and asked for 50,000 copies to be printed – the essay was coolly received at the time and for more than a century received scant critical attention. It is only during the past twenty years that 'Eureka' has been the subject of dispassionate scholarly analysis; today it is increasingly recognised as a work of intellectual integrity and imaginative power, a remarkable *tour de force* in which he exercised to the full both his visionary sweep and his extra-ordinary analytical gifts.

The essay is an attempt to summarise within a single philosophical framework a theory of the nature of the physical universe.[8] Drawing upon the principles of Newton, Kepler and Laplace, he postulates a mechanistic though continually evolving universe. In his concept time and space are both finite; matter was formed from nothingness, i.e., it was created, and ultimately the universe would reach a 'state of progressive collapse' when matter would cease to exist and the universe would therefore come to an end. The fundamental principle in his vision was 'complete *mutuality* of adaptation.... that absolute *reciprocity of adaptation* which is the idiosyncracy of the Divine Art. ...' The concept embraced not only the physical world and the time-space continuum but also the nature of man himself. Indeed 'Eureka' can be regarded as the final statement of a 'central view of the imagination'[9] which underlay all his work in both prose and verse and to which he remained consistent throughout his life. It is essentially a vision of a totally symmetrical universe, a universe in which the harmonious order that characterises it is seen as 'a plot of God'. It follows from this notion that man must reproduce this symmetry in his individual life, *that the creation of the effect of unity* must be an integral part of the poet's function. Poe regarded 'harmony, proportion, beauty and perfection' as synonymous terms[10] and in all his critical writings insisted on the central validity of unity of effect. Applied to literature, then, this philosophy meant that the primary concerns of a work of poetry or prose were to create a sense of harmony and to give aesthetic pleasure; *meaning*, in the sense of a didactic purpose, was subordinate to this central concern.

It is significant that in the Preface to 'Eureka' Poe stated:

I offer this Book of Truths, not in its character of Truth-Teller, but for the Beauty that abounds in its Truth; constituting it true.... I present the composition as an Art-Product alone: – let us say as a Romance; or, if I be not urging too lofty a claim, as a Poem.... it is as a Poem only that I wish this work to be judged after I am dead.

The words 'If I be not urging too lofty a claim' are highly significant, for in his terms there could be no higher praise than to regard the work as a poem. Indeed 'Eureka' can be fully understood in the context of his life and achievements only if one appreciates the central importance in his scheme of things of the search for unity, for harmony, for symmetry. Whether the work is regarded as a philosophical treatise to be interpreted literally, or as a myth, a poetic vision, will continue to exercise the minds of scholars for generations to come. What can be said with certainty is that in 'Eureka' Poe felt he had summarised his philosophy of life and art in a composition of total consistency and beauty, and that beyond this he had nothing further of substance to add. After its publication (New York, March 1848) only eighteen months of life remained to him.

* * * * *

Though his reputation as a storyteller and poet has tended inevitably to overshadow his achievement as essayist and critic, Poe's accomplishment in the latter fields remains impressive and coherent. Though the body of his work is less substantial than that of his contemporaries Emerson and Thoreau its range is remarkably wide. When one takes into account his major critical essays 'The Poetic Principle' and 'The Philosophy of Composition', his astute assessments of writers as diverse as Dickens and Hawthorne, his numerous analytical and deductive articles, the book reviews extending over a decade, and the mass of aphorisms and short essays collected together in the 'Marginalia', one returns to Poe with renewed admiration and respect. In his own fields he was an essayist of uncommon ability, observing the literary and intellectual world of his day and assessing it with insight and compassion. He was in a true sense a 'man of letters', the first complete man of letters to arise from the United States.

Part VI

THE POETRY

The Poetry

Throughout his literary career Poe regarded himself as first and foremost a poet and only secondarily a writer of short stories. He had turned to the writing of fiction when he realised that his earnings from poetry would be insufficient for his modest needs, but in the last analysis he felt this was a distraction from his central artistic concerns. For him the writing of poetry was 'not a purpose, but a passion'.[1]

During his lifetime four slim volumes of his verse were published: *Tamerlane and Other Poems* (1827), *Al Aaraaf, Tamerlane and Minor Poems* (1829), *Poems* (1831) and *The Raven and Other Poems* (1845). These collections contain in all some fifty poems, most of them short in length but of impressive beauty and power. The bulk of his poetry was written by 1831, when he was twenty-two, and during the remainder of his life his energies in this field – with a few notable exceptions – were devoted to the revision and improvement of his existing work rather than to the composition of new poems. Lewis Chase, in his interesting study *Poe and his Poetry*, has commented:

Although he relied upon initial inspiration as instinctively as other singers, the time and attention he devoted to revision, his method of subjecting each word to unrelenting scrutiny, and of publishing the revised version as often as he got a chance in newspapers, magazines, and in new editions, renders the whole of his work a veritable encyclopaedia, or rather a unique laboratory of poetic craft . . .. He is the type *par excellence* of the pertinaceous quest for technical perfection.[2]

Two examples must suffice here as illustrations of this continual process of revision. In the original version of 'To One in Paradise' (1834) the beautiful final verse concludes with the lines:

In what ethereal dances,
By what Italian streams.

In the final version, published twelve years later, this has been amended to:

In what ethereal dances,
By what eternal streams.

This is clearly an improvement both technically and poetically and expresses the *effect* he is seeking to convey – the idea of supernal beauty – with absolute perfection. A more extended illustration of the transition from first draft to final text occurs in 'A Dream Within a Dream'. Here the opening lines of the second verse went through the following process of alteration:

I am standing 'mid the roar
Of a weather-beaten shore [1829]

I was standing 'mid the roar
Of a wind-beaten shore [1831]

I stand amid the roar
Of a surf-tormented shore [1849]

We are so familiar with the final version, which is of course the text found in all copies of his poetry today, that we tend to overlook the long process of revision of which it is the result. Poe was, as we have seen, a compulsive reviser and his approach to his art, from first to last, was one of intense seriousness.

*   *   *   *   *

Tamerlane and Other Poems is an apprentice work, as he himself seems to have quickly acknowledged, although it remains a remarkable achievement for a youth of eighteen. Despite the unevenness of the poems it contained it is possible to discern in this poorly printed booklet numerous indications of the mature Poe and the first crude statement of themes which were to dominate his imagination throughout his career – regret for lost childhood, lament for the world of the imagination, the conflict between romantic passion and material ambition, and a sense of alienation from his fellow men.

'Tamerlane' itself, which Poe considerably shortened in the revision of 1829, tells of a narrator who abandons the happiness of his home and loved one in his quest for material ambition. Returning to his home, having achieved his worldly desires, he finds that the girl he loved is dead. He realises that his ambitions of material gain were a delusion and that for their sake he has not only lost his beloved but also his poetic imagination. This simple, almost trite, story is framed in heavily romantic language which owes much to Byron, perhaps the strongest single influence on the early poetry. But it is possible to discern beneath the Byronic trappings of 'Tamerlane' and the other verses themes of alienation and loneliness which were of direct relevance to his own life.

A fact which has to be continually taken into account in any assessment of Poe and his work is that, in contrast to his contemporaries at school and university, his origins were obscure and lowly. He must have regarded himself from an early age as a 'lost soul' (he was, to use a modern term, an 'outsider') and his life of forty years was beset with unhappiness and misfortune. It is this spiritual loneliness, this sense of being an outcast, which gives to much of his poetry a quality of sadness. In an early poem, 'Alone', which scholars assert was written as early as 1829 or 1830,[3] he gives perfect expression to this feeling of alienation:

> From childhood's hour I have not been
> As others were – I have not seen
> As others saw – I could not bring
> My passions from a common spring –
> From the same source I have not taken
> My sorrow – I could not awaken
> My heart to joy at the same tone –
> And all I lov'd – I lov'd alone.

In the same poem occur the lines:

> Then – in my childhood – in the dawn
> Of a most stormy life – was drawn
> From ev'ry depth of good and ill
> The mystery which binds me still . . .
> And the cloud that took the form
> Of a demon in my view.

It is not difficult to detect in these verses Poe's early
awareness of his own distinctive strengths and weaknesses,
those psychic qualities which together constituted his 'demon'.
He was, as we have seen, a deeply divided character: his entire
life could be described as a case study in contrasts. Born in
poverty of wandering actor parents, he was brought up in the
home and milieu of a wealthy Virginia gentleman; an American citizen by birth he spent much of his most impressionable
years in the older culture of England and Scotland; identified
with New England by his birthplace (Boston) he spent the
remainder of his life in antipathy to all that New England and
its literary circles stood for; temperamentally romantic and
imaginative, he saw himself as a coldly analytical reasoner
solving problems by the dispassionate use of intellect; the first
professional American man of letters, his whole life was spent
in a struggle against poverty and critical indifference. Viewed
against this background his poems assume a special and
deeper significance. From first to last, from 'Tamerlane' to
'Ulalume', they are the product of a tortured personality, a
man divided against himself, a man who, finding life intolerable, sought refuge in a series of womb-like images: the
whirlpool, the pit, the vault, the premature grave.

His second volume *Al Aaraaf, Tamerlane and Minor Poems*
contains, in addition to 'Al Aaraaf' (an ambitious work in
which Poe sought to express in abstract form his philosophy
that beauty and truth are one and the same) a number of
verses which testify to his growing self-confidence as a poet
and his increasing awareness of his own strengths. It is
important to bear in mind that the word 'minor' in the title is
meant to suggest brevity rather than insignificance: the
poems, while short, are notable for their rhythmic qualities

and the influence of his year's sojourn in South Carolina. There is, for example, 'Fairy-land', with its delicately evoked picture of a fairy kingdom, and 'Sonnet – To Science', one of the earliest statements of his view that poetry had to be conceived and experienced as a 'passion' rather than an abstract study.

A continually recurring theme in the poetry, as in the short stories, is the quest for eternal perfection as personified by a feminine character of rare beauty. Just as Ligeia, Eleonora and Berenice symbolised for Poe the elusive beauty he had found and lost in the person of Virginia Clemm, so Annabel Lee, Helen, Eulalie and Lenore personified for him his *idée fixe* of departed love, of happinesses transitorily experienced but never to be tasted again. This theme was already evident in his work as early as 1829 and is discernible in such poems as 'The bowers whereat, in dreams, I see' and 'I saw thee on thy bridal day'. Significant also in this early work is the mood of dream-like melancholy, of sadness at the passing of lost happiness, exemplied in such poems as 'A Dream':

In visions of the dark night
I have dreamed of joy departed –
But a waking dream of life and light
Hath left me broken-hearted.

It would be easy to dismiss Poe's early poetry as adolescent posturings, as the heavily imitative outpourings of a young man striving to express a series of inchoate ideas. Certainly the early work is open to criticism on these grounds. Yet on a deeper level it can be seen to be the rudimentary statement of a philosophical attitude of profound relevance to the twentieth century: that of the utter loneliness of man. Poe was in fact an existentialist long before the term was invented: he was one of the first writers to show an awareness of the terrifying implications of man's consciousness and to discuss themes and ideas which have become almost commonplace in our own time – annihilation, withdrawal from the self, mental disorder, and premonition of death.

Poems, published by Elam Bliss in 1831, marks a considerable advance in range and power. In the preface Poe commented: 'Believing only a portion of my former volume to be worthy of a second edition – that small portion I thought it as well to include in the present book as to republish by itself. I have therefore herein combined 'Al Aaraaf' and 'Tamerlane' with other poems hitherto unprinted.' The volume contains a number of poems of unusual imaginative power, including some which have placed him among the foremost poets of the world. Such compositions as 'The Sleeper', 'The City in the Sea', 'The Valley of Unrest' and 'To Helen' have earned for him a justified reputation as an artist whose work is characterised by a remote, strange beauty and a gift for mystical expression.

'The Sleeper' is a meditation on a theme to which he returned in such stories as 'Ligeia' and 'Berenice' – that of the beautiful female, now dead, whose corpse holds a fatal attraction to the beholder:

> The lady sleeps. Oh, may her sleep,
> Which is enduring, so be deep!
> Heaven have her in its sacred keep! ...
> My love, she sleeps. Oh, may her sleep,
> As it is lasting, so be deep!

This poem, one of the most *atmospheric* of all his works – it is rivalled only by 'Ulalume' in its careful building up of a mystic aura of reverence – is acknowledged by many critics as one of his finest compositions. It is among his most feelingly written rhapsodies on the theme of the departed beloved and one in which he experimented fruitfully with rhythmic and atmospheric forms.

'To Helen', which includes the frequently quoted lines 'To the glory that was Greece/And the grandeur that was Rome.', was inspired by Mrs. Jane Stith Stanard, the mother of his school companion Robert (Bobby) Stanard. She was by all accounts a woman of great beauty, graciousness and charm, and Poe described her years later as 'the first ideal love of my soul'. In the poem Poe likens her to Helen of Troy and himself to a 'weary, wayworn wanderer' borne home after a journey across the 'desperate seas' of life. The *idea* conveyed by the poem, that of the isolation of the narrator consequent upon the loss (or inaccessibility) of his beloved, was never handled better by Poe. 'To Helen' consists of but three verses of five lines each and has the deceptive appearance of simplicity. In fact it is one of the most frequently and carefully revised of all his poems: from its first appearance in 1831 to the final text of 1845 it passed through a complex process of revision and polishing before Poe was satisfied. It remains one of his most perfect expressions of idealised love and one which, had he written nothing else, would have earned him a place in anthologies of great poetry.

'The Raven', the poem by which Poe is most renowned in the English-speaking world, owed its origins to a review of *Barnaby Rudge* which he composed for *Graham's Magazine* (February 1841). In the course of this review he commented significantly on the symbolical importance of the raven in Dickens's novel:

> The raven, too, intensely amusing as it is, might have been made, more than we now see it, a portion of the conception of the fantastic Barnaby. Its croakings might have been *prophetically* heard in the course of the drama. Its character might have performed in regard to that of the idiot, much the same part as does, in music, the accompaniment in respect to the air . . .. Yet between them there might have been wrought an analogical resemblance, and although each might have existed apart they might have formed together a whole which would have been imperfect in the absence of either.

He seems to have brooded on the idea at intervals for a period of three or four years, discussing the concept with his friends as the poem painstakingly evolved through a series of drafts. It received its final form in the farmhouse in which Poe, Virginia and Mrs. Clemm were staying on the Bloomingdale Road, New York. The furnishings of this house, which was situated in those days in a semi-rural setting, actually included a 'pallid bust of Pallas' which has since become inseparably associated with Poe and as immortal as Holmes's Persian slipper or Alice's looking-glass. Writing in a fever of inspiration, confident that the poem would prove to be his popular masterpiece, he blended together the ingredi-

ents which, he sensed, would create a unique and unforgettable work of art: the antique, romantic furnishings of the
room, the insistent refrain of the raven, the eternal theme of
regret for the lost beloved and, fusing all into a cohesive
whole, his skill in achieving an atmosphere of haunting
melancholy.

That 'The Raven' has a direct relevance to the circumstances of his own life there can be no doubt. It combines
two themes which were central to his emotional experience –
the idea of the beautiful, dead, 'lost Lenore' and the lonely,
bookish man who is confronted with his own inner self in the
form of the raven. His wife Virginia was dying of tuberculosis
and had been visibly ailing since the beginning of 1842.
Brooding on this fact he seems to have realised that the ideal,
romantic love he had visualised in youth had eluded him
throughout his life and would continue to do so. Always, he
sensed, he was doomed to be frustrated in his quest for a
perfect emotional response; it was a dream which evaded his
grasp each time he sought to achieve it. As the truth of this
came home to him there must have been moods when despair
almost overwhelmed his life. Writing to Poe apropos 'The
Raven', his friend R. H. Horne commented shrewdly that in
his view 'the poet intends to represent a very painful condition
of mind, as of an imagination that was liable to topple over into
some delirium or an abyss of melancholy, from the continuity
of one unvaried emotion'. Artistically and rhythmically 'The
Raven' is an impressive piece of work – a haunting composition which has become one of the most quoted poems in the
language, notable for its insistent metre and the unforgettable
effect of its refrain – but it is much more than a technical
accomplishment. Its logical presentation (it is almost alone in
his poetry in telling a story) has tended to obscure the deep
emotion with which it is written. It would be a remarkable
poem by any standards, whoever had composed it: but as the
work of Poe it is of intense psychological and emotional
interest.

On its publication in January 1845 its success was instantaneous. It attracted more attention than anything he had
written previously, even eclipsing 'The Gold-Bug'. Writing to
his friend F. W. Thomas some months later he claimed 'The
bird beat the bug all hollow'. It earned for him little financial

reward but widespread critical and popular respect in the
United States and England. Elizabeth Barrett Barrett, to
whom he dedicated his volume *The Raven and Other Poems*,
wrote to him: 'Your 'Raven' has produced a sensation, a 'fit
horror' here in England. Some of my friends are taken by the
fear of it and some by the music. I hear of persons haunted by
the 'Nevermore', and one acquaintance of mine who has the
misfortune of possessing a 'bust of Pallas' never can bear to
look at it in the twilight'.

After the publication of 'The Raven' Poe enjoyed two years
of comparative literary success before his life began to
disintegrate. With the death of Virginia in January 1847 his
world began to collapse about him, yet, despite his personal
unhappiness and his worsening health, he continued to write
poetry of great artistic merit. To these final years belong some
of his most enduring work, including 'Ulalume', 'Annabel
Lee' and 'Eldorado'. These last poems, so characteristic of his
mind and vision, are a fitting conclusion to his life and
achievement as a creative artist.

'Ulalume', written in the aftermath of his wife's death, is an
elaborate meditation on the contrast between pure love (Dian)
and lust (Astarte). It takes the form of a debate between the
poet and his inner self, and in this sense makes an interesting
comparison with his story 'William Wilson', which is also a
fantasia on the theme of the divided self. The interplay in
'Ulalume' between noble and ignoble passion and the poet's
own soul (Psyche) renders the work extremely significant,
particularly when placed in context against the background of
his life. At the end of the poem the narrator confronts the
tomb of his departed love, Ulalume, but realises that only
death can reunite him with her and with the lost happiness she
symbolises. The poem has been described as 'allegorised
autobiography'[4] and indeed it is not difficult to see in these
haunting, melancholy verses a prolonged cry of anguish at
Virginia's demise:

And I cried – "It was surely October
On this very night of last year
That I journeyed – I journeyed down here,
That I brought a dread burden down here:

On this night of all nights in the year,
Ah, what demon has tempted me here?
Well I know, now, this dim lake of Auber,
This misty mid region of Weir:
Well I know, now, this dank tarn of Auber,
This ghoul-haunted woodland of Weir."

'Auber' and 'Weir' both seem to be names coined by Poe; they do not correspond to actual locations but rather to regions of the mind, to moods and emotions with which he became increasingly familiar as he neared the end of his life. The phrase 'ghoul-haunted woodland', so redolent of the mental torment he must have undergone during these years, is one of the most revealing ever to fall from his pen. Throughout 1848–9 his life was an almost unceasing struggle against poverty and ill-health, a struggle in which, even in the depths of unhappiness and frustration, he clung passionately to his artistic integrity. Yet there must have been moods and phases during this time when the 'ghoul-haunted woodland' of mental agony overwhelmed him and he succumbed to despair.

'Annabel Lee', published on the day of his death, is a moving and beautifully written tribute to Virginia Clemm. That Virginia is the subject of the poem seems clear from a number of references, including the lines 'I was a child and she was a child,' and 'But our love it was stronger by far than the love/Of those who were older than we,/Of many far wiser than we.' The simplicity and beauty of the poem – it is widely held to be the simplest and sweetest of his ballads, is frequently anthologised and has even been set to music – is deceptive, for it is in reality one of his most deeply felt compositions and conceals an emotional intensity rare in the canon of his work. It was begun as early as the summer of 1846, i.e., even *before* Virginia's death. Poe must have been aware that his young wife was dying and in 'Annabel Lee' he set out to write a lyrical meditation on her life and death and all she had meant to him. There are few more moving lines in all his verse than the avowal of the narrator of his immutable love:

And neither the angels in heaven above,
Nor the demons under the sea,

Can ever dissever my soul from the soul
Of the beautiful Annabel Lee:

For the moon never beams, without bringing me dreams
Of the beautiful Annabel Lee;
And the stars never rise, but I feel the bright eyes
Of the beautiful Annabel Lee

In his final emendation Poe altered the last line from 'In her tomb by the side of the sea' to the artistically more satisfying 'In her tomb by the sounding sea'. It is significant that the sea is a continual presence throughout the poem: a reminder of his fascination with the sea and sea lore. The insistent, musical rhythm of the verses is akin to the endless sound of the waves on Sullivan's Island and, in a deeper sense, is symbolic of the undying love of the narrator for the dead maiden. Sarah Helen Whitman thought that Virginia was the only woman Poe truly loved, and 'Annabel Lee' can be seen as an eloquent testimony of that assertion. The composition of it must have cost him agonies, both in the literary and the emotional sense. It bears all the hallmarks of careful revision (from a purely rhythmical standpoint it is perhaps the most perfect of all his poems) and critics are unanimous in praise of its symmetry and charm. But emotionally it is in many ways his most revealing work. Not only does it describe one of his most characteristic themes – the premature death of a beloved maiden – but it is permeated with images and symbols which recur again and again in his writings: a lonely sepulchre, tormented dreams, a love beyond earthly understanding and, finally, union with the dead bride in the tomb.

There is a persistent though unverified legend that 'Eldorado' was the last of Poe's poems to be written. For this reason it is customary to place it as the last item in selections of his verse and it forms an appropriate coda to his life's work. It was written at a time (spring 1849) when the Californian gold rush was very much in the news and when the elusive pursuit of gold was simultaneously being treated by him in the form of prose ('Von Kempelen and his Discovery'). The poem, however, cannot be understood fully in the literal sense as a commentary on the chimerical search for wealth, but should be seen rather as a reflection of Poe's lifelong search for

emotional and intellectual fulfilment. Seen in these terms
'Eldorado' is a wholly Poe-esque composition which contains
within it a number of pertinent indicators to his state of mind
during the closing months of his life. As with 'Annabel Lee',
the apparent simplicity of its style has tended to conceal its
underlying seriousness of purpose. In the first verse, for
example, occur the significant lines

Gaily bedight,
A gallant knight,
In sunshine and in shadow,
Had journeyed long,
Singing a song,
In search of Eldorado.

The phrase 'in sunshine and in shadow' is interesting and
may be taken as symbolic of Poe's fluctuating moods of hope
and disillusionment. At the beginning of 1849 the tide in his
literary fortunes seemed to be turning in his favour and he
wrote enthusiastic letters to his friends describing his rising
hopes. Writing to Mrs. Annie Richmond he commented: 'So
you see that I have only to keep up my spirits to get out of all
my pecuniary troubles'. But such moods were to be short-
lived. Soon afterwards some of the manuscripts on which he
had taken great pains, including 'Landor's Cottage', were
rejected and he turned with bitterness and sorrow to the
writing of 'Hop-Frog'. In a sense his entire life, including his
childhood and adolescence, was spent 'in sunshine and in
shadow'. Indeed there can be few writers who have described
so feelingly the depths of despair and aboulia to which the
human spirit is subject.

In the second and third verses there are two different and
intriguing uses of the word 'shadow'. The first refers to a
shadow which fell over the heart of the knight

as he found
No spot of ground
That looked like Eldorado.

In this sense 'shadow' is clearly meant to signify disap-
pointment: an emotion of regret and unease at the realisation

that the land of his dreams shows no sign of attainability. In the second reference the knight encounters a 'pilgrim shadow' who advises him on the course of his journey. Here 'shadow' is employed in the sense of a reflected image, an inseparable companion, just as 'William Wilson' is the *shadow* of his namesake. This return to the theme of the divided self which we have also noted in 'Ulalume' is peculiarly apposite in this, his last poem. It should be noted that the pilgrim is encountered at the precise moment when the knight's strength fails him: his realisation that he is not alone comes simultaneously with an awareness that his life is ebbing away. The pilgrim urges the knight to pursue his quest

Over the Mountains
Of the Moon,
Down the Valley of the Shadow

The phrase 'down the valley of the shadow', with its biblical connotations of death and the approach of death, is a telling reminder of Poe's consciousness of his own fatal illness. The line also contains the implication that if, at the end of the knight's long journey, Eldorado is to be reached at last, it can only be so after undergoing a testing experience of unhappiness and travail.

The poem is utterly characteristic of Poe in its air of simple, almost naive hope, its theme of elusive aspirations, and its continual emphasis on the theme of *seeking*. Notice that the knight does not at any stage of the poem actually attain his goal. Always he is searching in quest of his elusive, beckoning ideal; even at the end he is still journeying on, urged by the pilgrim shadow to 'Ride, boldly ride, if you seek for Eldorado.' Thus it is that in this short poem Poe gave expression, consciously or otherwise, to a series of *leit-motifs* which had haunted his life and art for two decades – the alternation between hope and despair which yielded the deepest extremes of happiness and sorrow and yet produced his finest work; the realisation that, despite his utmost efforts, his dreams of literary recognition would elude him to the end; the preoccupation with the idea of a double, a shadow which would follow him throughout his life; and the awareness of his own impending demise. All these elements are fused together in 'Eldorado' to create a work of abundant energy and fascination: a poem which is in both a literal and an allegorical sense a last testament.

*   *   *   *   *

T. S. Eliot said of him: 'It will seem puzzling that, with such a narrow range of emotion, such a lack of ordinary human passion and sympathy, the author of so few poems should be more than a minor poet. But, in the first place, his poetry is original. That is to say, his vision of life, though limited, was peculiar and coherent and his idiom unmistakeable. He takes you into a world different from that of any other poet . . . . once his poems have become part of your experience, they are never dislodged'.[5] Eliot was surely right to stress the memorable, indeed unforgettable quality of the best of his poetry. A poem such as 'A Dream within a Dream', 'To Helen', 'Dreamland' or 'The Bells', once read is never forgotten. It persists in the memory and, such is the power of Poe's rhythm and language, can frequently be recited long after the original reading. The strength of the poetry is his ability to convey deep emotion – grief, as in 'Annabel Lee'; affection, as in 'To My Mother' (a touching tribute to Maria Clemm); romantic love, as in 'To Helen'; regret, as in 'To One in Paradise'; alienation, as in 'Alone' – in language of the utmost ease and fluency. Their very simplicity is deceptive and has led some critics to dismiss them as too facile. In fact careful study of the poems and attention to their language and construction reveals in almost every case a care in composition amounting to the meticulous.

The limitations of Poe's poetry are obvious and critics have not been slow to point them out.[6] There is, first, the *unreality* of his themes and settings: with few exceptions his verses depict scenes and situations remote from worldly experience. In the sharpest contrast to Wordsworth, Keats and Longfellow his poems contain little reference to scenes of natural beauty or to normal human experience. Instead, they are concerned with an imaginative and emotional world divorced from everyday considerations; it is as if they occupy a dimension of their own, a world characterised by sorrow, reverie and remorse. Then, the *narrow range* of his work. Not only are his poems limited in scope – only fifty or so in total, many of them brief – but their range of subject is surprisingly small. They are concerned predominantly with moods and feelings peculiarly apposite to himself – a preoccupation with the loss of the visionary world of childhood, regret at the passing of a loved one, alienation from mankind, a yearning after the intangible. These are all of course Romantic attitudes which he derived, consciously or otherwise, from his wide reading and his lonely introspection, but they had a strong and direct relevance to the circumstances of his life. Finally, his poetry is open to criticism on the grounds of its *artificiality*. As each of the poems is the final result of a long process of careful revision, it can be argued that, whilst technically they are difficult to fault, they lack the spontaneity of great poetry: that, in essence, Poe was an accomplished *technician* rather than an artist.

To these criticisms Poe would have replied that the supreme aim of poetry (as of music) is the creation of beauty, and that all other considerations had to be subordinated to this. Indeed his poetry can only be fully understood and appreciated when measured against his own criteria. However deficient his verses may be by orthodox critical standards there is no denying their utter sincerity nor the intense feeling with which they were composed. No claim is made that all the poetry is of equal merit for this is manifestly not so. In his poetry, as in his prose, Poe was an uneven writer and some of the poems – for example, 'A Valentine' and 'Evening Star' – are not of the same standard as his finest work. But when writing at the height of his powers he was capable of composing verse which is read and appreciated wherever poetry is read. In such poems as 'The Raven', 'To Helen', 'Annabel Lee' and 'Alone' he made a permanent contribution to English literature and moreover gave expression to moods and emotions which struck a deeply responsive chord in the minds of his readers. His was an original and disturbing voice.

Part VII

CHARACTERS AND LOCATIONS IN POE'S FICTION

Characters and Locations in Poe's Fiction

This section consists of an alphabetically arranged dictionary of the characters and places occupying a significant role in the short stories and romances.

The following abbreviations are used throughout:

Amontillado	*The Cask of Amontillado*
Angel	*The Angel of the Odd*
Arnheim	*The Domain of Arnheim*
Assignation	*The Assignation*
Balloon	*The Balloon-Hoax*
Blackwood	*How to Write a Blackwood Article*
Breath	*Loss of Breath*
Burial	*The Premature Burial*
Crowd	*The Man of the Crowd*
Devil	*Never Bet the Devil Your Head*
Eiros	*The Conversation of Eiros and Charmion*
Fay	*The Island of the Fay*
Four Beasts	*Four Beasts in One; The Homo-Camelopard*
Gold-Bug	*The Gold-Bug*
Heart	*The Tell-Tale Heart*
Jerusalem	*A Tale of Jerusalem*
Kempelen	*Von Kempelen and His Discovery*
Landor	*Landor's Cottage*
Literary	*The Literary Life of Thingum Bob, Esq.*
Maelström	*A Descent Into the Maelström*
Masque	*The Masque of the Red Death*
Mesmeric	*Mesmeric Revelation*

Monos	*The Colloquy of Monos and Una*
Morgue	*The Murders in the Rue Morgue*
Mummy	*Some Words with a Mummy*
Oblong	*The Oblong Box*
Pendulum	*The Pit and the Pendulum*
Perverse	*The Imp of the Perverse*
Pest	*King Pest*
Pfaall	*The Unparalleled Adventure of One Hans Pfaall*
Predicament	*A Predicament*
Purloined	*The Purloined Letter*
Pym	*The Narrative of Arthur Gordon Pym*
Ragged Mountains	*A Tale of the Ragged Mountains*
Rodman	*The Journal of Julius Rodman*
Rogêt	*The Mystery of Marie Rogêt*
Scheherazade	*The Thousand and Second Tale of Scheherazade*
Spectacles	*The Spectacles*
Tarr	*The System of Doctor Tarr and Professor Fether*
Thou Art	*Thou Art the Man*
Used Up	*The Man that was Used Up*
Usher	*The Fall of the House of Usher*
Valdemar	*The Facts in the Case of M. Valdemar*
Wilson	*William Wilson*
Words	*The Power of Words*

AGATHOS. One of the interlocutors in *Words*, he discourses with Oinos on the effect of motion in the universe.

AINSWORTH, HARRISON. Historical novelist (1805–82) and author of *Jack Sheppard, The Tower of London, Windsor Castle* and *Old St. Pauls*. He is one of the passengers in the balloon which crosses the Atlantic in three days and the alleged author of part of the subsequent account. *Balloon*.

ALLAMISTAKEO, COUNT. An Egyptian nobleman who is embalmed while in a cataleptic trance. Centuries later his mummified body is brought back to life by the application of an electric current. The Count proceeds to discourse upon the achievements of the ancient civilisations, drawing unfavourable comparisons with nineteenth-century ideas of 'progress'. *Mummy*.

ANTIOCH. The setting for a satirical short story placed in the remote past in which Poe comments upon attitudes to cruelty and inhumanity. *Four Beasts*.

ARNHEIM. The mysterious domain created by the wealthy landowner Ellison, in which he lives in solitude surrounded by a beautiful landscape. The domain is essentially a romantic longing for the pastoral way of life Poe had glimpsed during boyhood and at intervals during his adult life. (Cf. Hervey Allen, *Israfel: The Life and Times of Edgar Allan Poe*, pp. 251–2, 587. Cf. also John Fowles, *The Magus*, including especially the Foreword to the revised edition, 1977, and *Daniel Martin* by the same author). *Arnheim*.

BARNARD, AUGUSTUS. Son of a sea captain and a close friend of Arthur Gordon Pym. He smuggles Pym aboard the brig *Grampus*, setting sail for the South Seas on a whaling voyage. The crew of the ship mutiny and it is severely damaged in a storm. Augustus displays great bravery and loyalty in harrowing circumstances, but eventually dies of malnutrition and the effects of a wound sustained at the hands of the mutineers. *Pym*.

BARNARD, CAPTAIN. A sea captain of considerable experience, commander of the brig *Grampus* which sets sail from Nantucket in June 1827 bound for the South Seas. During the voyage the crew plan a mutiny; the captain is overpowered and set adrift in a small boat, together with four others, in the vicinity of the Bermuda Islands. His son Augustus, left behind on the brig, consoles himself with the hope that his father has been able to reach land. *Pym*.

BEDLOE, AUGUSTUS. A singularly tall and thin man, stooping, with long and emaciated limbs and a broad, low forehead. He suffers from neuralgic attacks and has for many years been attended by a physician. One day he embarks upon a long ramble among the mountains, in the course of which he imagines himself to be transported to the Indian city of Benares in the year 1780. *Ragged Mountains*.

BERENICE. Of 'gorgeous yet fantastic beauty', Berenice is loved by her cousin Egaeus; the two are brought up together in the home of Egaeus's father. Her cousin proposes marriage, but before the nuptials can be arranged Berenice dies of epilepsy. Egaeus covets Berenice's beautiful teeth and, violating the grave, extracts them – only to realise that she is still alive. *Berenice.*

BOB, THINGUM. Son of Thomas Bob, Esq., a barber in the city of Smug. Thingum aspires to literary pretensions, and, as a result of an ingenious forgery, becomes in time editor of the *Goosetherumfoodle*. At the end of his life he composes his literary reminiscences as a bequest to posterity. *Literary.*

BON-BON, PIERRE. A *restaurateur* 'of uncommon qualifications' who has a certain reputation as an amateur philosopher. While at work on one of his manuscripts the Devil calls on him and they get drunk together. The Devil explains that he cannot keep himself supplied with his favourite diet: the souls of philosophers. Bon-Bon offers his, only to be met with an evasive reply. *Bon-Bon.*

CHARLESTON. A city in South Carolina which Poe knew well from his army service at Fort Moultrie a few miles away. His mother, Elizabeth Arnold, had taken part in theatrical performances in the city, and Poe had visited Charleston as a small child in 1811. At the time of his sojourn in the area (1827–8) the city was a major port, and he incorporated much of his knowledge of the Charleston sailing packets in his story of the young husband who takes with him on board ship the embalmed body of his wife. *Oblong.*

CHARMION. One of the interlocutors in Eiros, he discourses with Eiros on the cosmic disaster which has overtaken the earth.

D———, THE MINISTER. An unscrupulous man, he dares all things, 'those unbecoming as well as those becoming a man'. He steals a compromising letter from the royal apartments and hides it in a letter-rack in his hotel. Dupin knows him to be both a mathematician and a poet and, from his knowledge of the Minister and his understanding of the latter's methods of reasoning, is able to deduce that the document is concealed in an obvious place – so obvious, in fact, that the police had not thought of searching there. Dupin outwits him by retrieving the letter and substituting a facsimile. *Purloined.*

DAMMIT, TOBY. The son of a left-handed mother who flogged him unmercifully. As he grows up 'his precocity in vice was awful'; he becomes addicted to gambling and to the phrase 'I'll bet the Devil my head.' One day he insists he can leap over a stile and uses his time-worn phrase as a wager. The Devil takes him up on the boast and as a result he is deprived of his head. *Devil*.

DELUC, MADAME. The owner of a roadside inn close to the bank of the river Seine. She claims to have heard screams in the vicinity of the inn on the day of Marie Rogêt's death and describes a gang of miscreants seen in the area. Her subsequent confession to the police confirms the details of Dupin's process of deduction (who is suspicious of her evidence throughout) regarding the method of the crime and the identity of the murderer. *Rogêt*.

DUPIN, C. AUGUSTE. A young detective who is extremely interested in the solving of abstruse problems by a process of ratiocination and deduction. He is 'of an excellent, indeed of an illustrious family, but, by a variety of untoward events, had been reduced to such poverty that the energy of his character succumbed beneath it, and he ceased to bestir himself in the world, or to care for the retrieval of his fortunes'. Books are his sole luxuries. He lives in apartments with the narrator (unnamed) whom he first encounters in a library in the Rue Montmartre. They soon become firm friends and Dupin astonishes his companion with the wide extent of his reading and his vivid imagination. Dupin demonstrates that it is possible to unravel the most baffling problems by the application of reason. *Morgue, Rogêt, Purloined*.

EDGARTON. The boyhood home of Arthur Gordon Pym. In recalling his school days in Edgarton – 'He sent me, at six years of age, to the school of old Mr. Ricketts, a gentleman with only one arm, and of eccentric manners' – Poe is apparently referring to the school he attended at Richmond (circa 1814). The name 'Edgarton' is an obvious pun on Poe's own name. *Pym*.

EDINBURGH. The setting for a farcical short story in which the narrator, the Signora Psyche Zenobia, is beheaded by the minute hand of the cathedral clock. (Poe passed briefly through Edinburgh on his way from Scotland to London in October 1815). *Predicament*.

EGAEUS. The descendant of 'a race of visionaries', he grows up with his cousin Berenice in his ancestral home. He suffers from ill health and moods of gloom, in contrast to the energy and grace of his cousin. He proposes marriage to her but before the nuptials can be arranged she dies of epilepsy. He has become obsessed with the beauty of her teeth, and, after her death, extracts them, realising too late that in reality she was not dead but simply in an epileptic trance. *Berenice*.

EIROS. One of the interlocutors in *Eiros*, she discourses with Charmion on the cosmic disaster which has overtaken the earth.

ELEONORA. Brought up with her cousin in seclusion in the Valley of the Many-Coloured Grass, Eleonora is fragile and innocent and dies while still a young girl. Her cousin, who has loved her dearly, vows eternal faithfulness to her memory, but later falls in love with and marries another girl. A voice tells him that he is absolved from his vows to Eleonora. *Eleonora*.

ELLISON. 'From his cradle to his grave a gale of prosperity bore my friend Ellison along.' Ellison's life is guided by four basic principles: free exercise in the open air, the love of woman, contempt for ambition, and an object of unceasing pursuit. On coming of age he inherits a fortune from a wealthy namesake and devotes the remainder of his life to the study of landscape gardening and to the creation of a *domain* perfect in every detail and of surpassing beauty. *Arnheim*.

FISHERMAN, THE. He and his two brothers are caught in the Maelström whirlpool whilst fishing off the coast of Norway. His brothers perish by drowning but the fisherman avoids being drawn into the whirlpool by lashing himself to a barrel. The experience so terrifies him that his hair is changed from raven black to white and he is not recognised by the companions who rescue him. Three years later he describes his experience to the narrator. *Maelström*.

FORTUNATO. An Italian nobleman noted for his connoisseur-ship in wine. He was a man 'to be respected and even feared' but antagonises his enemy Montresor to such an extent that Montresor vows revenge. Under the pretext of showing him a cask of Amontillado, his avenger lures Fortunato into the family catacombs and walls him up alive in a crypt. *Amontillado*.

FRANCE. The setting for a number of the short stories,

including *Morgue, Rogêt, Purloined,* and *Tarr.* For a study of Poe's influence on French literature and thought see Patrick F. Quinn, *The French Face of Edgar Poe,* (Southern Illinois University Press, 1957).

FROISSART, NAPOLEON BONAPARTE. Son of M. Froissart and Mademoiselle Croissart, of Paris. He possesses 'what nine-tenths of the world would call a handsome face', but is extremely short-sighted. Because of his vanity, however, he refuses to wear spectacles. He is tricked into marrying his own great-great-grandmother and changes his name to Simpson in order to receive a large inheritance. *Spectacles.*

G———, MONSIEUR. The Prefect of the Parisian police. He visits Dupin in his apartments and begs him to retrieve a letter purloined from the royal family by the Minister D———. There is 'nearly half as much of the entertaining as of the contemptible about the man', and Dupin gives him a hearty welcome. One of the Prefect's characteristics is to label as 'odd' anything which is beyond his comprehension. *Purloined.*

GOODFELLOW, CHARLES. A respected citizen of Rattle-borough and the alleged close friend of Barnabas Shuttleworthy, he has a reputation for honesty and integrity on the strength of his ingenuous face 'which is prover-bially the very "best letter of recommendation".' He murders Shuttleworthy and conceals the corpse; the crime is discovered and the corpse is sent to his home in the guise of a box of wine. *Thou Art.*

GUY, CAPTAIN. Captain of the Schooner *Jane Guy* of Liverpool. He was 'a gentleman of great urbanity of manner, and of considerable experience in the southern traffic, to which he had devoted a great portion of his life'. He rescues Pym and Dirk Peters from the crippled *Grampus* and proceeds on a trading voyage to the South Seas. On reaching the island of Tsalal he befriends the natives but falls victim to their deception, perishing with almost the whole of his crew in an avalanche engineered by the islanders. *Pym.*

HERMANN, JOHAN. A university student who has a reputation for deep metaphysical thinking but is in reality a fool. He has great renown as a duellist and, after an argument, challenges the Baron Ritzner Von Jung to a duel. The baron recommends Hermann to read a passage from an apparently learned (but in reality meaningless) treatise on etiquette, and as a result honour is satisfied. *Mystification*.

HOP-FROG. A professional jester at the court of a king, he is a crippled dwarf possessed of considerable physical strength. He is in love with the dwarf Trippetta. When Trippetta is insulted by the King, Hop-Frog vows revenge; he persuades the king and his ministers to dress as orang-outangs, tars and feathers them, then sets them alight. He and the girl then effect their escape through the sky-light. *Hop-Frog*.

HUNGARY. The setting for *Metzengerstein*, the first of Poe's short stories to be published. The tale, which is a pastiche of the horror tales of E. T. A. Hoffman (1776–1822), concerns the long-standing feud between the inhabitants of the Castle Berliftzing and the Palace Metzengerstein.

JERUSALEM. The setting for a humorous short story in which Poe caricatures the kind of far-fetched narrative then popular with readers of *Blackwood's Magazine*. *Jerusalem*.

JUPITER. The negro servant of William Legrand. He had been employed by the Legrand family in its days of wealth but could not be induced 'neither by threats nor by promises, to abandon what he considered his right of attendance upon the footsteps of his young "Massa Will" '. He considers himself to be Legrand's guardian and, when his master becomes obsessed with the hunt for Captain Kidd's buried treasure, fears for Legrand's sanity. *Gold-Bug*.

KEMPELEN, VON. The inventor of a method of transforming lead into gold. He is 'short and stout, with large, *fat*, blue eyes, sandy hair and whiskers, a wide but pleasing mouth, fine teeth, and I think a Roman nose'. He is arrested by the police in the midst of his experiments but refuses to divulge the secret of his method. He is related to the hoaxer Baron Wolfgang Von Kempelen whom Poe had exposed in 'Maelzel's Chess-Player'. *Kempelen*.

LACKOBREATH, MR. On the morning after his wedding he discovers that he has lost his breath. After a series of adventures, in the course of which he is mistaken for a corpse, he eventually succeeds in regaining his voice from his neighbour Windenough who had inadvertently appropriated it. *Breath*.

LANDOR. The tenant of a picturesque cottage romantically situated in a beautified landscape in one of the New York river valleys. He is 'civil, even cordial in his manner', and receives his visitor with great courtesy; his visitor is overwhelmed with the beauty of the cottage and of its surrounding scenery: 'Its marvellous *effect* lay altogether in its artistic arrangement *as a picture.' Landor*.

LEGRAND, WILLIAM. A recluse who lives upon Sullivan's Island, near Charleston, occupying his time in fishing and entomology. He is 'well educated, with unusual powers of mind, but infected with misanthropy, and subject to perverse moods of alternate enthusiasm and melancholy'. He discovers a memorandum containing, in secret code, directions for locating treasure hidden many years previously by Captain Kidd. Legrand solves the code through an ingenious process of ratiocination and, together with his negro servant, Jupiter, and the narrator, succeeds in finding and recovering the treasure. *Gold-Bug*.

LEGS. A tall, thin seaman, the close companion of Hugh Tarpaulin. He has 'high cheek-bones, a large hawk-nose, retreating chin, fallen under-jaw, and huge protruding white eyes'. He and his companion embark on a drunken exploration of plague-ridden London and encounter a group of eccentrics claiming to be King Pest the First and his entourage. Legs and Tarpaulin decline to take part in their undignified rituals and, after a fracas in which the self-proclaimed royal family is routed, succeed in making their escape. *Pest*.

L'ESPANAYE, MADAME. An elderly lady who tells fortunes for a living and is also reputed to have a private income. She and her daughter Mademoiselle Camille L'Espanaye occupy apartments in the Rue Morgue in the Quartier St. Roch, Paris. They are both murdered by an escaped orang-outang; the mother by decapitation and the daughter by strangulation. *Morgue*.

LIGEIA, LADY. Tall of stature, slender, and with features of haunting loveliness, Ligeia is worshipped by a man who dotes on her incomparable beauty and learning. She is deeply proficient in both classical and modern languages and in physical and mathematical science; 'in beauty of face no maiden ever equalled her'. When Ligeia dies her husband is overwhelmed with grief and cannot remove her image from his mind. *Ligeia*.

LONDON. Poe lived at various addresses in London during the
years 1815–20 and the city figures prominently in a number
of his short stories. He stayed first in furnished lodgings at
47 Southampton Row, Bloomsbury (October–December
1815); then at the Misses Dubourg's boarding school at 146
Sloane Street, Chelsea (early 1816–summer 1817); and
finally at Manor House School, Church Street, Stoke
Newington (autumn 1817–June 1820).

A romanticised description of the Manor House School
and of Stoke Newington, 'a misty-looking village of England, where were a vast number of gigantic and gnarled
trees, and where all the houses were excessively ancient', is
to be found in *Wilson*, which should be closely studied for its
insight into the impact of England upon the young Poe.

From the summer of 1817 to June 1820 John Allan lived
in lodgings at 39 (now renumbered 83) Southampton Row,
where Poe frequently visited him at weekends and school
holidays. This is the house mentioned in *Frenchman* as '39,
Southampton Row, Russell Square, Parish o' Bloomsbury,'
as the residence of Sir Pathrick O'Grandison.

Crowd is set entirely in London, the action ranging widely
over London streets and scenes. The narrator observes in
passing that there is a vast difference between 'a London
populace and that of the most frequented American
city'.

Pest is also set in London, the action commencing in an
ale-house in 'the parish of St. Andrews' (Holborn) and
continuing in a range of scenes set 'in those horrible
regions, in the vicinity of the Thames, where, amid the
dark, narrow, and filthy lanes and alleys, the Demon of
Disease was supposed to have had his nativity'.

MAELSTRÖM. A dangerous whirlpool off the coast of Norway,
the setting for the short story *Maelström*. Poe had in fact
never visited the area, but derived the materials for the tale
from literary sources.

MAILLARD, MONSIEUR. The superintendent of a private lunatic asylum in the South of France who seeks to administer
the asylum on enlightened principles. On becoming insane
himself he is admitted as a patient. The patients then seize
power and imprison the keepers in undergound cells. M.
Maillard keeps up the pretence that he is the superintend-

ent but after a month the keepers free themselves and order is restored. *Tarr*.

MENTONI, MARCHESA APHRODITE. The young wife of a Venetian nobleman, she is described as 'the adoration of all Venice – the gayest of the gay – the most lovely where all were beautiful'. She is loved by a wealthy Englishman but her husband, discovering her secret, poisons both her and her lover. *Assignation*.

METZENGERSTEIN, BARON FREDERICK. Son of a Hungarian nobleman who inherits a vast estate whilst still a young man. He sets fire to the castle of a neighbouring family with whom there has been intense rivalry for centuries, and as a result his enemy the Count dies. Metzengerstein becomes obsessed with a splendid horse which has escaped from the Count's burning stables and rides it to death amidst the blazing ruins of his own Palace. *Metzengerstein*.

MONOS. One of the interlocutors in *Monos*, he discourses with Una on life after death.

MONTRESOR. An Italian nobleman who vows revenge on his antagonist Fortunato after many insults and humiliations. He accosts Fortunato at the height of the carnival season and, under the pretext of showing him a cask of Amontillado, lures him into the family catacombs and walls him up alive in a crypt. The family arms of the Montresors is 'a huge human foot d'or, in a field azure; the foot crushes a serpent rampant whose fangs are imbedded in the heel,' with the motto *Nemo me impune lacessit* [No one provokes me with impunity]. *Amontillado*.

MORELLA. A deeply learned woman, well versed in philosophy and literature, she marries a man who becomes her pupil. They gradually become estranged and eventually Morella dies in childbirth, her daughter also being given the same name. The daughter bears an uncanny resemblance to her mother and when, years later, she too dies, no trace of the first Morella can be found in the family tomb. *Morella*.

NANTUCKET. A coastal area of Massachusetts, some eighty miles from Boston. Poe may have visited the area in the course of his journey from Richmond to Boston in the spring of 1827.

Nantucket was the birthplace of Arthur Gordon Pym and

from here he set sail in the brig *Grampus* on his epic voyage to the polar regions. *Pym*.

OINOS.   One of the interlocutors in *Words*, she discourses with Agathos on the effect of motion in the universe.

PARIS.   The setting of three of Poe's tales of ratiocination and the home of the detective, C. Auguste Dupin.

Dupin and the narrator first meet 'at an obscure library in the Rue Montmartre' and decide to live in lodgings together in a ruined mansion in the Faubourg St. Germain. The detective then investigates the gruesome murders of a mother and daughter in the fourth storey of a house in the Rue Morgue.

Dupin's next case concerns the murder of a young girl found floating in the Seine, close to the Quartier of the Rue Saint Andrée and the secluded neighbourhood of the Barrière due Roule. The third and final detective story opens in Dupin's library, No. 33 Rue Dunôt, Faubourg St. Germain, and concerns the theft of an incriminating letter from the D——— (unnamed) Hotel. *Morgue, Rogêt, Purloined*.

PETERS, DIRK.   Son of a fur trader and an Indian squaw, Peters was 'one of the most purely ferocious-looking men I ever beheld'. He is short in stature and has bowed arms and legs, but possesses great physical strength and courage. As a member of the crew of the *Grampus*, he befriends Augustus Barnard and Pym and joins forces with them against the mutineers. After the death of Augustus he survives privation and illness and has many adventures with Pym, including a journey to the South Seas and to the polar regions. Later he returns to the United States and settles in Illinois. *Pym*.

PFAALL, HANS.   A Bankrupt bellows-mender from Rotterdam who, in order to escape from debt concocts an ingenious hoax in which he alleges that the explanation for his disappearance five years previously is that he had journeyed to the moon in a balloon. His creditors, he claims, were accidentally killed during the ascent from earth. *Pfaall*.

PONNONNER, DOCTOR.   A notable Egyptologist who is given permission to unswathe a mummy preserved in a museum. To the Doctor's amazement the mummy comes back to life when an electric current is applied to it. *Mummy*.

PRISONER, THE. Sentenced to death during the Spanish Inquisition, he is banished to a dungeon cell in Toledo. He explores his cell and finds that there is a deep circular pit in the centre of the floor from which rats emerge. Awakening after a drugged sleep he finds himself bound to a wooden framework and that a razor-sharp blade is slowly descending upon him. With considerable ingenuity he succeeds in escaping from the death intended for him and is rescued by French soldiers as he is about to fall into the pit. *Pendulum*.

PROSPERO, PRINCE. A happy, dauntless and sagacious ruler who, during a plague, retires to a remote abbey with one thousand knights and dames in order to escape the effects of the pestilence. During a masked ball an unknown masquerader, dressed to resemble a victim of the plague, confronts the Prince and kills him. *Masque*.

PYM, ARTHUR GORDON. Son of a trader in sea stores at Nantucket. As a youth he becomes acquainted with the son of a sea captain and becomes extremely interested in seafaring tales. With the connivance of his friend he becomes a stowaway aboard the brig *Grampus*, setting sail for the South Seas on a whaling voyage. After many incredible adventures and privations, in the course of which he journeys to the polar regions, he returns to New York and writes an account of his experiences. He dies suddenly, leaving the manuscript uncompleted. *Pym*.

RAGGED MOUNTAINS. A chain of hills in the vicinity of Charlottesville, Virginia, which Poe knew well from his days as a student at the University of Virginia. He frequently wandered alone among the hills and, years later, he made the area the setting for an ingenious short story in which a young man, Augustus Bedloe, is transposed from the mountains to the Indian city of Benares in the year 1780. *Ragged Mountains*.

RATTLEBOROUGH. The scene of the murder of Mr. Barnabas Shuttleworthy and of the dramatic confrontation with his assassin, Charles Goodfellow. *Thou Art*.

RODMAN, JULIUS. A young Kentucky traveller who embarks on a trapping expedition up the Missouri in the 1790s. At the conclusion of his adventures he returns to Virginia and writes an account of his expedition in the form of a diary. *Rodman*.

ROGÊT, MARIE. The only daughter of the widow Estelle Rogêt. The mother and daughter keep a *pension* until Marie's beauty comes to the attention of a perfumer, Monsieur Le Blanc, who asks her to join him as an assistant. Marie disappears in mysterious circumstances and her body is eventually found floating in the Seine. The murder is solved by C. Auguste Dupin who, from a detailed examination of newspaper reports, is able to deduce the identity of her assassin. *Rogêt*.

ROTTERDAM. The scene of the opening and closing sequences of *Pfaall*. Hans Pfaall hovers over Rotterdam in a balloon and throws overboard a letter addressed to the burgo-master, Superbus Von Underduk. The letter proves to be an ingeniously contrived request to be pardoned for the death of his creditors.

SAILOR, THE. The owner of the orang-outang which murders Madame L'Espanaye and her daughter. He is 'a tall, stout, and muscular-looking person, with a certain dare-devil expression of countenance, not altogether unprepossessing'. He acquires the ape in Borneo and brings it to Paris, intending to sell it, but the animal escapes. *Morgue*.

SCHEHERAZADE. The relater of the stories in 'The Arabian Nights', and elder daughter of the Vizier of Persia. She astounds her husband the king by describing to him a number of nineteenth-century inventions and dis-coveries – including railways, calculating machines, the telegraph, etc. – but he refuses to believe her. She is executed at the conclusion of her narrative. *Scheherazade*.

SHUTTLEWORTHY, BARNABAS. A wealthy and respectable citizen of Rattleborough who disappears under mysterious circumstances. It transpires that he has been murdered by his 'bosom friend' Charles Goodfellow, who has then concealed the corpse. The crime is discovered and the corpse is sent to the murderer's home in the guise of a box of wine. *Thou Art*.

SMITH, BRIGADIER-GENERAL JOHN A. B. C. The hero of the Bugaboo and Kickapoo campaign, a tall, distinguished figure with a commanding presence. He has jet-black hair and whiskers, beautiful teeth, and a melodious voice. An interviewer seeks a meeting with him in order to learn more of his military exploits, but discovers to his chagrin that everything about the General is false – his legs, arms, hair, teeth, even his voice. *Used Up.*

STOKE NEWINGTON. *See* LONDON.

SULLIVAN'S ISLAND. A small island off the coast of Charleston, South Carolina, the scene of much of the action of *Gold-Bug.* Poe knew the island and its surrounding area intimately from the year he spent on garrison duty at Fort Moultrie (November 1827–December 1828). The island is notable for its interesting population of birds and insects.

TARPAULIN, HUGH. A young seaman, the close companion of 'Legs'. He is four feet in height and 'a pair of stumpy bow-legs supported his squat, unwieldy figure, while his unusually short and thick arms, with no ordinary fists at their extremities, swung off dangling from his sides like the fins of a sea-turtle'. He and his companion embark on a drunken exploration of plague-ridden London and encounter a group of eccentrics purporting to be King Pest the First and his family. Tarpaulin and 'Legs' refuse to humour them and, with great presence of mind, succeed in routing the self-proclaimed monarchy. *Pest.*

TOLEDO. A town in central Spain and one of the strongholds of the Spanish Inquisition (c.1490–1835), in the dungeons of which an un-named prisoner is incarcerated. The prisoner succeeds in escaping from a razor-sharp pendulum which slowly descends on him, only to narrowly avoid death in a deep pit in the centre of his cell. *Pendulum.*

TOO-WIT. Chief of the island of Tsalal. When the schooner *Jane Guy* visits the island on a trading voyage he appears to welcome the crew in a friendly manner and pretends to fall in with their proposals for trade and peaceful co-operation. In reality, however, he and the islanders plan deception and they engineer an avalanche which kills almost the entire crew. (The name *Too-wit* is Hebrew in origin and means, literally, 'to be dirty'.) *Pym.*

TREVANION, LADY ROWENA. After the death of the Lady Ligeia she marries Ligeia's husband, although she does not love him and dreads his moodiness. Some months after the marriage Rowena is stricken with fever and dies. Her husband, still obsessed with the image of Ligeia and mentally confused as a result of taking opium, imagines that her corpse is that of his first wife. *Ligeia*.

TRIPPETTA. A young female dwarf, the companion of Hop-Frog, a court jester. She is 'of exquisite proportions, and a marvellous dancer'. She and Hop-Frog are drawn together by their diminutive size and by the fact that both had been forcibly removed from their homes and sent as presents to the king. When Trippetta is humiliated by the king Hop-Frog devises a terrible revenge on him and his court. The two dwarfs then effect their escape and return to their own country. *Hop-Frog*.

TSALAL. An island in the South Seas, one of a group of eight islands governed by a common king. The island is inhabited by black savages who are totally ignorant of civilisation. When the schooner *Jane Guy* visits the island on a trading voyage the natives appear to welcome the crew; Pym sees through their deception, however, and concludes that they are among 'the most barbarous, subtle, and bloodthirsty wretches that ever contaminated the face of the globe'. (The name *Tsalal* is of Hebrew origin and means, literally, 'to be dark'.) *Pym*.

UNA. One of the interlocutors in *Monos*, she discourses with Monos on life after death.

USHER. The family mansion and domain of the House of Usher. Poe gives no clue as to its supposed location, beyond the fact that it is situated in the midst of 'a singularly dreary tract of country'. The house may well have been suggested by one of the ruined colonial mansions he saw in Carolina whilst serving in the army. *Usher*.

USHER, MADELINE. The beloved sister of Roderick Usher, 'his sole companion for long years, his last and only relative on earth'. She and her brother live together in a decaying mansion; she is, however, dying of a wasting disease. After her death her brother arranges to have the body temporarily entombed, but later realises to his horror that she has been buried alive. *Usher*.

USHER, RODERICK. A member of a very ancient family noted for their 'peculiar sensibility of temperament, displaying itself, through long ages, in many works of exalted art', he lives in the House of Usher with his sister, Madeline, as his sole companion. He occupies his time in painting and music, and in reading obscure works of theology and history. Feeling ill and depressed, he invites a boon companion of boyhood to stay with him for a sojourn of some weeks; during this sojourn his sister dies of a wasting disease. At the height of a storm Usher and his companion realise to their horror that Madeline is not dead but has been placed in the tomb while still living. Usher dies of fright when his sister enters the room in which he is listening to a gothic narrative and collapses upon him. *Usher*.

VALDEMAR, ERNEST. A Franco-Polish writer, translator of Schiller and Rabelais, who lives in Harlem, New York. He is notable for 'the extreme spareness of his person' and for 'the whiteness of his whiskers, in violent contrast to the blackness of his hair – the latter, in consequence, being very generally mistaken for a wig'. He is a good subject for mesmeric experiments and is hypnotised on numerous occasions over a period of seven months, throughout which time he appears to be slowly dying of tuberculosis. When at length the hypnotist attempts to awaken him from his mesmeric trance, Valdemar insists that he is dead and his body disintegrates. (The name 'Valdemar' is literally val-de-mar: the valley of death). *Valdemar*.

VALLEY OF THE MANY-COLOURED GRASS. The home of Eleonora and her cousin who live together in the valley for fifteen years before falling in love with one another. After the death of Eleonora the valley becomes unbearable to her cousin because of its memories of lost happiness, and he leaves it never to return. *Eleonora*.

VANKIRK, MR. A dying man who is hypnotised during the closing stages of tuberculosis. During his final trance he speculates upon life after death and on the nature of matter. After Vankirk's death rigor mortis sets in almost at once and the hypnotist poses the question: 'Had the sleep-walker, indeed, during the latter portion of his discourse, been addressing me from out the region of the shadows?' *Mesmeric*.

VENICE. The scene of the encounter between a wealthy Englishman and the wife of a nobleman, the Marchesa Aphrodite Mentoni. The Marchesa is first described as she stands alone beneath the covered archway known as the

Ponte di Sospiri (the Bridge of Sighs). The action of the story then moves to the palazzo of her lover, 'one of those huge structures of gloomy yet fantastic pomp, which tower above the waters of the Grand Canal in the vicinity of the Rialto'. *Assignation*.

VON JUNG, BARON RITZNER. A member of a noble Hungarian family, every member of which was 'more or less remarkable for talent of some description'. An unhandsome man with angular, harsh features, he devotes his life to the study of the science of mystification. He is challenged to a duel by a gentleman who has considerable renown as a duellist, but Von Jung extricates himself from this situation by citing an obscure passage in a learned treatise on the subject, knowing that his opponent will not understand it but will be too proud to admit this. *Mystification*.

WILSON, WILLIAM. The descendant of 'a race whose imaginative and easily excitable temperament has at all times rendered them remarkable', he grows up self-willed and a prey to uncontrollable passions. He becomes a pupil at the school of the Reverend Dr. Bransby in 'a large, rambling Elizabethan house, in a misty-looking village of England' [the Manor House School, Stoke Newington] and while there becomes embarrassed by the rivalry of another scholar bearing the same Christian name and surname as himself. Wilson becomes increasingly irritated by his namesake, who copies him in every particular and seizes every opportunity of annoying and humiliating him. At last, exasperated beyond endurance, he kills his antagonist with a sword, only to realise that in doing so he has destroyed his better self. *Wilson*.

WINDENOUGH. The neighbour of Mr. Lackobreath and an admirer of his neighbour's wife. He is a tall, thin man, disliked by Mr. Lackobreath since the latter is short and corpulent. When his friend loses his breath Mr. Windenough inadvertently acquires it and is assumed to have epilepsy. *Breath*.

WYATT, CORNELIUS. A young artist who possesses 'the ordinary temperament of genius, and was a compound of misanthropy, sensibility, and enthusiasm'. His beautiful and accomplished wife dies as he is about to embark on a sea voyage; he arranges to have the corpse embalmed and conveyed on board ship as merchandise. When it becomes necessary to abandon the ship due to storm damage he refuses to leave his wife's body and is drowned. *Oblong.*

ZENOBIA, SIGNORA PSYCHE. Deeply concerned at the poverty of contemporary thought and literature, Zenobia interviews the editor of *Blackwood's Magazine* seeking advice on how to compose an article for that journal. He gives her many hints on the sensational ingredients and pretensions to scholarship required by his readers. During a visit to Edinburgh she climbs the clock tower of the cathedral and is beheaded by the minute hand. *Blackwood* and *Predicament.*

Appendix: Film Versions

The following is a list of the principal film versions of Poe's stories.

1. FILM ADAPTATIONS

1909   *The Life of Edgar Allan Poe.* Biograph. Directed by D. W. Griffith. Starring Herbert Yost as Poe.

1909   *The Sealed Room.* Biograph. Starring Henry B. Walthall and Marion Leonard. Based on 'The Cask of Amontillado'.

1909   *Lunatics in Power.* Edison Studios. Based on 'The System of Doctor Tarr and Professor Fether'.

1910   *The Pit and the Pendulum.* Ambrosio Films.

1910   *Hop Frog the Jester.* Ambrosio Films.

1912   *The Raven.* Eclair. Starring Guy Oliver as Poe.

1912   *The Bells.* Edison Studios. Directed by George Lessey.

1913   *The Lunatics.* Eclair. Directed by Robert Saidreon. Starring Henri Gouget and Monsieur Bahier. Based on 'The System of Doctor Tarr and Professor Fether'.

1913   *The Pit and the Pendulum.* Solax Film Company. Starring Darwin Karr and Blanche Cornwall.

1914   *The Avenging Conscience.* Directed by D. W. Griffith. Starring Henry B. Walthall and Blanche Sweet. Based on 'The Tell-Tale Heart'.

1915   *The Raven.* Essanay. Directed by Charles J. Brabin, starring Henry B. Walthall as Poe.

1929   *The Fall of the House of Usher.* Directed by Jean Epstein.

1931   *The Mystery of Marie Roget.* Universal.

1932   *The Murders in the Rue Morgue.* Starring Bela Lugosi.

1934   *The Black Cat.* Universal. Directed by Edgar G. Ulmer.

Starring Boris Karloff and Bela Lugosi.

1935   *The Raven.* Starring Boris Karloff and Bela Lugosi. An amalgam of Poe's short stories.

1942   *The Loves of Edgar Allan Poe.* Fox. Starring John Shepperd and Morton Lowry. Directed by Harry Lachman.

1942   *The Mystery of Marie Roget.* Universal.

1942   *The Tell-Tale Heart.* Metro Goldwyn Mayer. Directed by Jules Dassin.

1947   *The Fall of the House of Usher.* Starring Kaye Tendeter.

1950   *The Tell-Tale Heart.* Starring Stanley Baker.

1951   *The Man with a Cloak.* Metro Goldwyn Mayer. Directed by Fletcher Markle. Starring Joseph Cotton as Poe, and Barbara Stanwyck. Based on 'The Gentleman from Paris' by John Dickson Carr.

1954   *Phantom of the Rue Morgue.* Starring Karl Malden.

1954   *The Tell-Tale Heart.* UPA. Cartoon, narrated by James Mason.

1956   *Manfish.* Based on 'The Tell-Tale Heart' and 'The Gold-Bug'.

1960   *The Tell-Tale Heart.* Starring Laurence Payne.

1960   *The House of Usher.* American International Pictures. Directed by Roger Corman. Starring Vincent Price, Mark Damon and Myrna Fahey.

1961   *The Pit and the Pendulum.* American International Pictures. Directed by Roger Corman. Starring Vincent Price, John Kerr and Barbara Steele.

1962   *Poe's Tales of Terror.* American International Pictures. Directed by Roger Corman. Starring Vincent Price, Basil Rathbone and Peter Lorre. Based on 'The Black Cat', 'The Facts in the Case of M. Valdemar', and 'Morella'.

1962   *The Premature Burial.* American International Pictures. Directed by Roger Corman. Starring Ray Milland.

1963   *The Raven.* American International Pictures. Directed by Roger Corman. Starring Vincent Price, Boris Karloff and Peter Lorre.

1964   *The Haunted Palace.* American International Pictures. Directed by Roger Corman. Starring Lon Chaney and Vincent Price.

1964   *Castle of Terror.* Vulsina-Woolner. Directed by Anthony Dawson. Starring Barbara Steele, George Riviera and Henry Kruger.

1964 *The Masque of the Red Death.* American International Pictures. Directed by Roger Corman. Starring Vincent Price and Hazel Court.

1965 *The Tomb of Ligeia.* American International Pictures. Directed by Roger Corman. Starring Vincent Price and Elizabeth Shepherd.

1965 *War Gods of the Deep.* (Also known as *City Under the Sea*) American International Pictures. Directed by Jacques Tourneur. Starring Vincent Price, Tab Hunter and Susan Hart. Based on 'The City in the Sea'.

1968 *The Conqueror Worm.* American International Pictures. Directed by Michael Reeves. Starring Vincent Price.

1968 *Torture Garden.* Amicus. Directed by Freddie Francis. Based on stories by Robert Bloch, including 'The Man Who Collected Poe'.

1969 *Spirits of the Dead.* American International Pictures. Directed by Roger Vadim, Louis Malle and Frederico Fellini. Starring Peter and Jane Fonda, Brigitte Bardot and Terence Stamp. Based on 'Metzengerstein', 'William Wilson' and 'Never Bet the Devil Your Head'.

1969 *The Oblong Box.* American International Pictures. Directed by Gordon Hessler. Starring Vincent Price and Christopher Lee.

1970 *Cry of the Banshee.* American International Pictures. Directed by Gordon Hessler. Starring Vincent Price.

1971 *Murders in the Rue Morgue.* American International Pictures. Directed by Gordon Hessler. Starring Jason Robards, Lilli Palmer and Herbert Lom.

1974 *The Spectre of Edgar Allan Poe.* Cinerama. Directed by Mohy Quandor. Starring Robert Walker Jr. as Poe and Mary Grover as Lenore.

2. FICTION

1952 *The Opener of the Crypt* by John Jakes. A sequel to 'The Cask of Amontillado'. Included in *The Boris Karloff Horror Anthology*, (London: Everest Books, 1975).

1967 *The Man Who Collected Poe* by Robert Bloch. Written for the film *Torture Garden*. A pastiche of 'The Fall of the

House of Usher'. Included in *Tales of a Monster Hunter*, selected by Peter Cushing. (London: Futura Publications, 1978).

1969　*The Man Who Called Himself Poe*. Edited by Sam Moskowitz. An anthology of short stories inspired or suggested by Poe's fiction.

1978　*The Poe Papers: A Tale of Passion*. by N. L. Zaroulis. (London: W. H. Allen,). A convincingly written and well researched narrative describing an attempt by a Poe collector to retrieve a collection of letters exchanged between Poe and Mrs. Nancy Richmond.

1978　*Poe Must Die* by Marc Olden (London: Hamlyn). A melodrama set in London and the United States in the year 1848 and describing Poe's attempts to foil a mysterious black magician searching for the Throne of Solomon.

References

The following abbreviations are used throughout:

Allen   Hervey Allen, *Israfel: The Life and Times of Edgar Allan Poe* (New York: Farrar and Rinehart, 1934).
Bittner   William Bittner, *Poe, A Biography* (London: Elek Books, 1963).
Carlson   Eric W. Carlson (ed.), *The Recognition of Edgar Allan Poe* (University of Michigan Press, 1966).
Chase   Lewis Chase, *Poe and his Poetry* (London: Harrap, 1913).
Hoffman   Daniel Hoffman, *Poe Poe Poe Poe Poe Poe Poe* (London: Robson Books, 1972).
Lloyd   J. A. T. Lloyd, *The Murder of Edgar Allan Poe* (London: Stanley Paul, 1931).
Pym   Edgar Allan Poe, *The Narrative of Arthur Gordon Pym*.
Rans   Geoffrey Rans, *Edgar Allan Poe* (Edinburgh: Oliver & Boyd, 1965).
Sinclair   David Sinclair, *Edgar Allan Poe* (London: Dent, 1977).
Stern   Philip Van Doren Stern (ed.), *The Portable Edgar Allan Poe* (New York: Viking Press, 1945).

THE LIFE OF EDGAR ALLAN POE

1. Allen, 85.
2. This letter, dated 19 March 1827, is quoted in full in Stern, 1–2.
3. Poe was probably suffering from an organic illness such as diabetes. Cf. Sinclair, 151–3.
4. For a full discussion of the relationship between Poe and Allan see Allen, chs III, VIII and XIII.
5. Sinclair, 36.
6. Stern, XVI.

POE'S LITERARY REPUTATION

1. The article is reproduced in its entirety in Carlson, 28–35.
2. 'The Question of Poe's Narrators', *College English*, XXV, December 1963,

pp. 177–81. Reproduced in Regan (ed.), *Poe: A Collection of Critical Essays*.
3. Walker, Ian M., 'Edgar Allan Poe'. *American Literature to 1900* (Sphere Books, 1975).
4. Quoted in Hubbell, Jay B., Introduction to *Tales and The Raven and Other Poems* (Columbus, Ohio: Charles E. Merrill Publishing Company, 1969).

THE SHORT STORIES

1. Lloyd, 71.
2. Rans, 76; Hoffman, 140–6.
3. Allen, 364.
4. Carlson, 172–6.
5. Allen, 299, 358.
6. William Legrand is described as 'well educated, with unusual powers of mind, but infected with misanthropy, and subject to perverse moods of alternate enthusiasm and melancholy'.
7. Bittner, 143.
8. The translation of *Le Grand Meaulnes* by Lowell Blair (New York: New American Library, 1971) has an interesting 'Afterword' by John Fowles which should be studied in this connection. Cf. also H. G. Wells's short story 'The Door in the Wall'.
9. See, for example, William J. Scheick, 'The Geometric Structure of Poe's "The Oval Portrait",' *Poe Studies*, vol. 11, no. 1, June 1978.
10. Bittner, 177.
11. Letter from Darley to Professor G. E. Woodberry, February 1884.
12. Allen, 454.
13. The letter is quoted in full on pp. 375–6 of Beaver (ed.), *The Science Fiction of Edgar Allan Poe* (London: Penguin Books, 1976).
14. Sinclair, 217.
15. Bittner, 185.
16. Mark Twain (1835–1910) declared that Poe's prose was 'unreadable', yet the influence of Poe upon his work can be plainly seen in such tales as 'The Facts Concerning the Recent Carnival of Crime in Connecticut' and in his humorous essays 'How I Edited an Agricultural Paper' and 'Curing a Cold'.
17. Cf. Poe's letter to James Russell Lowell, 2 July 1844.
18. Cf. Whipple, W., 'Poe's Two-Edged Satiric Tale', *Nineteenth Century Fiction*, vol. 9 (1954), pp. 121–33. See also *David Copperfield*, ch. LXI, for Dickens's satirical comments on 'the model system'.

THE ROMANCES

1. *Pym*, ch. 1.
2. Ibid., ch. 20. Cf. Wells's description of the Morlocks: 'those unpleasant creatures from below, these whitened Lemurs, this new vermin that had replaced the old . . . . inhuman and malign'. (*The Time Machine*, IX, X).
3. Cf. the concluding paragraphs of 'MS. Found in a Bottle'. See also Wells, *Experiment in Autobiography*, 97.

4. See Burton R. Pollin, 'Pym's *Narrative* in the American Newspapers: More Uncollected Notices', *Poe Studies* vol. 11, no. 1, June 1978.
5. See, for example, Harold Beaver, Appendix to the Penguin edition of *Pym* (Penguin Books, 1975).
6. Wells, *Experiment in Autobiography*, 97.
7. *Pym*, 20 and Wells, *Mr. Blettsworthy on Rampole Island*, ch. 3, § 9.
8. Ibid., ch. 3, § 10.
9. Wells to Huxley, 12 February 1928, quoted in Julian Huxley, *Memories* (Allen & Unwin, 1970).

ESSAYS AND CRITICISM

1. Bates, H. E., *The Modern Short Story: A Critical Survey* (Nelson, 1950).
2. Review of Hawthorne's *Twice-Told Tales*.
3. Stevenson, R. L., *Essays Literary and Critical*, 1923.
4. O'Grady, Hardress, Introduction to *Essays and Stories by Edgar Allan Poe* (Bell, 1914).
5. Allen, 490.
6. Allen, 463.
7. Cf. for example James Hilton's novel *Lost Horizon*, H. G. Wells's short story, 'The Door in the Wall', Alain-Fournier's *Le Grand Meaulnes*, and John Fowles's *Daniel Martin*.
8. It is interesting to note that H. G. Wells, who was influenced by Poe in many ways, also attempted at the end of his life to write a summary of his idea of the universe, *The Conquest of Time* (1942). Wells described this as 'a fairly lucid and consistent summary of modern ideas concerning the fundamentals and ultimates of existence'.
9. Rans, 18.
10. Poe, 'Men of Genius' (Marginalia).

THE POETRY

1. Preface, *The Raven and Other Poems*.
2. Chase, 26–7.
3. Tate, Allen, Introduction to *Edgar Allan Poe: Complete Poetry and Selected Criticism* (New York: New American Library, 1968).
4. Chase, 108.
5. Eliot, T. S., 'A Dream Within A Dream', *The Listener*, 25 February, 1943.
6. Cf. for example Aldous Huxley, 'Vulgarity in Literature', (1930) reprinted in Carlson, *The Recognition of Edgar Allan Poe* (Ann Arbor, 1970).

Select Bibliography

THE WORKS OF EDGAR ALLAN POE

The following editions are recommended:

The Complete Works of Edgar Allan Poe, edited by James A. Harrison, 17 volumes (New York: Thomas Y. Crowell, 1902). (The Virginia Edition.)

Tales of Mystery and Imagination, introduced by Padraic Colum. (London: J. M. Dent, 1908). (Everyman's Library: frequently reprinted.)

Essays and Stories by Edgar Allan Poe, selected with an Introduction by Hardress O'Grady. (Includes the whole of the 'Marginalia') (London: G. Bell, 1914).

The Complete Tales and Poems of Edgar Allan Poe, introduced by Hervey Allen. (New York: Random House, 1938).

The Complete Poems and Stories of Edgar Allan Poe with Selections from His Critical Writings 2 vols. Edited by A. H. Quinn and E. H. O'Neill. (New York, 1946).

The Portable Edgar Allan Poe, selected and edited with an introduction and notes by Philip Van Doren Stern. (New York: The Viking Press, 1945).

Edgar Allan Poe: Poems and Essays, introduced by Andrew Lang. (London: J. M. Dent, 1927). (Everyman's Library: frequently reprinted.)

Edgar Allan Poe: Selected Tales, edited with an introduction by Kenneth Graham. (Oxford University Press, 1967).

Selected Writings of Edgar Allan Poe, edited with an introduction by David Galloway. (Harmondsworth: Penguin Books, 1967).

The Complete Poetry and Selected Criticism of Edgar Allan Poe, edited by Allen Tate. (New York: New American Library, 1968).

The Narrative of Arthur Gordon Pym of Nantucket, edited with an introduction and commentary by Harold Beaver. (Harmondsworth: Penguin Books, 1975).

The Science Fiction of Edgar Allan Poe, collected and edited with an introduction and commentary by Harold Beaver. (Harmondsworth: Penguin Books, 1976).

Comic Tales of Edgar Allan Poe, edited with an introduction by Angus Wolfe Murray. (Edinburgh: Canongate Publishing, 1973).

Collected Works of Edgar Allan Poe; vol. I, Poems; vol. II. Tales and Sketches 1831–1842; vol. III, Tales and Sketches 1843–1849, edited by T. O. Mabbott (Cambridge, Massachusetts: Belknap Press of Harvard University Press, 1969–1978).

THE LETTERS

The Letters of Edgar Allan Poe, edited by John W. Ostrom. (Cambridge, Massachusetts: 1948). (revised edition, New York: Gordian Press, 1966). (There are two 'Supplements' in *American Literature*, XXIV [1952] and XXIX [1957].)

Edgar Allan Poe: Letters Till Now Unpublished. Introduction and commentary by Mary Newton Stanard. (Philadelphia, 1925).

BIBLIOGRAPHY

A Bibliography of First Printings of the Writings of Edgar Allan Poe, by C. F. Heartman, and J. R. Canny, (Hattiesburg, Mississippi, The Book Farm, 1940) (revised edition, 1943).

Bibliography of the Writings of Edgar A. Poe, by J. W. Robertson, 2 vols. (San Francisco, 1934).

BIOGRAPHY

Hervey Allen, *Israfel: The Life and Times of Edgar Allan Poe* (New York: Farrar and Rinehart, 1934). An extremely comprehensive, lavishly illustrated and generally reliable account of Poe's life and background. This biography is particularly valuable for the insight it affords into Poe's early life and the influence of his childhood upon his work and attitudes. The author was one of the foremost Poe scholars of the inter-war years and whilst later research has inevitably supplemented his biography on matters of detail the book remains a solid and perceptive introduction which is unlikely to be superseded.

Arthur Hobson Quinn, *Edgar Allan Poe: A Critical Biography* (New York, 1941). Now accepted as the definitive account of Poe's life and times, the biography has a place in literary history as one of the outstanding assessments of a major man of letters. If it has a weakness it is that it lacks objectivity, tending instead towards an uncritical approach towards the writer and his work. The scale and depth of this biography, however, make it an indispensable contribution to Poe studies.

William Bittner, *Poe: A Biography* (London: Elek, 1963). A highly readable and painstaking account of Poe's life and times, interspersed with apposite criticism of the poetry and prose. The author sets out to 'present his life from his point of view, showing his rationalisations and vacillations, his errors and flaws, as he might have been conscious of them', and in this intention he succeeds admirably. There is a useful appendix on 'the Poe controversies', i.e., the basic points on which scholarly opinion is divided.

Lettice Cooper, *The Young Edgar Allan Poe* (London: Max Parrish, 1964). An excellently written account of Poe's childhood and adolescence, covering in detail the years 1809–1827. Cast in the form of a fictional narrative, the book makes no claim to be a work of original scholarship: it is rather an attempt to convey the atmosphere of Poe's formative years and the impact upon him of his early friendships and experiences.

David Sinclair, *Edgar Allan Poe*. (London: Dent 1977). A wholly excellent and perceptive biography, illuminated throughout by penetrating insight and shrewd judgment. This remarkably balanced and invigorating appraisal is valuable not least for its insight into Poe's boyhood years in England; his temperament and basic attitudes; and his complicated medical history. The book, which has a useful bibliography of biographical and critical works, steers a middle course between idolatry and censoriousness.

Julian Symons, *The Tell-Tale Heart: The Life and Works of Edgar Allan Poe*. (London: Faber & Faber, 1978). This is a not entirely successful attempt to separate Poe's life from his work. The book makes no claim to be a work of original scholarship but it serves a useful function as an introduction to its subject written by a distinguished crime novelist. There is a comprehensive annotated bibliography.

CRITICISM

There is an immense literature of critical works on Poe, of which the following are likely to be found generally most valuable:

Lewis Chase, *Poe and his Poetry* (London: Harrap, 1913), edited with a preface by W. H. Hudson. This volume is one of a series, the intention of which is 'to interest the reader in the lives and personalities of the poets dealt with, and at the same time to use biography as an introduction and key to their writings'. An excellent introductory survey which places each poem in context against the background of Poe's life and circumstances.

Geoffrey Rans, *Edgar Allan Poe* (Edinburgh: Oliver and Boyd, 1965). (Writers and Critics series.) This compact volume is an immensely stimulating and important contribution to Poe scholarship. There are sections of erudite and succinct commentary on the criticism, the poetry and the fiction, and a helpful summary of modern critical works. The book is supplemented by an excellent bibliography of primary and secondary sources.

N. Bryllion Fagin, *The Histrionic Mr. Poe* (Baltimore: Johns Hopkins Press, 1949). An extremely interesting study of the histrionic aspects of Poe's temperament. The author argues convincingly that Poe was consciously histrionic in both his life and his works.

Daniel Hoffmann, *Poe Poe Poe Poe Poe Poe Poe* (London: Robson Books, 1972). An intensely idiosyncratic and lively reading of Poe written by a distinguished American poet and critic. The book is unfortunately marred by its excessive egotism and the fact that it ignores much previous Poe scholarship. The author does himself and his subject a disservice by deliberately writing in a colloquial style which is entirely inappropriate in a work of this nature.

Burton R. Pollin, *Discoveries in Poe* (Indiana: University of Notre Dame Press, 1970). This is a fascinating and erudite study of selected aspects of Poe's works. The author concentrates in particular on the influence of Victor Hugo upon Poe; on the influence of Byron and the Shelley-Godwin circle; the sources of 'Eleonora', 'To Zante' and 'Von Kempelen and His Discovery'; and his attempts to found a magazine of his own under the titles *The Penn* and *The Stylus*.

The work is a model of its kind. It is illuminated throughout by penetrating scholarship and is annotated with extensive references to original sources. The author demonstrates conclusively that, by a process of deduction similar to that employed by Poe himself in his tales of ratiocination, much can still be discovered about his works and the sources which inspired them. These discoveries in turn throw fresh light on his life and his literary methods.

Robert Regan (ed.), *Poe: A Collection of Critical Essays* (New Jersey: Prentice-Hall, 1967). (Twentieth Century Views series.) This is a collection of modern critical scholarship on Poe and his work, prefaced by a perceptive and stimulating introduction. The concentration is mainly upon the short stories, with the addition of essays dealing with Poe's 'philosophy of composition' and *The Narrative of Arthur Gordon Pym*. This useful and representative symposium is a most valuable contribution to Poe studies.

Eric W. Carlson (ed.), *The Recognition of Edgar Allan Poe* (University of Michigan Press, 1970). This is a useful collection of selected criticism from 1829 to the present, much of it unobtainable elsewhere. It includes the infamous

'Ludwig' article by Rufus Griswold, and critiques of Poe by such diverse hands as Baudelaire, Dostoevsky, Henry James, Bernard Shaw, D. H. Lawrence and T. S. Eliot. Unfortunately there is no index.

ADDITIONAL RECOMMENDATIONS

J. A. T. Lloyd, *The Murder of Edgar Allan Poe* (London: Stanley Paul, 1931).

Killis Campbell, *The Mind of Poe* (Cambridge, Massachusetts: 1933).

William Sansom, 'Edgar Allan Poe', in *Pleasures Strange and Simple* (London: Hogarth Press, 1953).

Patrick F. Quinn, *The French Face of Edgar Poe* (Carbondale, Illinois: 1957).

Ian M. Walker, 'Edgar Allan Poe', in *American Literature to 1900 (Sphere History of Literature in the English Language, vol. 8)*. (London: Sphere Books, 1973).

Edward Wagenknecht, *Edgar Allan Poe: The Man Behind the Legend* (New York: Oxford University Press, 1963).

Peter Haining, *The Edgar Allan Poe Scrapbook* . (London: New English Library, 1977).

Index

Ainsworth, Harrison 130–1, 170
Alain-Fournier 72
Allan, Frances Valentine 5, 6, 12, 13, 14, 22
Allan, John 5–18 *passim*, 22
Allen, Hervey xi, 66, 68
Arnold, Elizabeth *see* Poe, Elizabeth Arnold

Baltimore 14, 16, 21, 32, 62–3, 76, 88
Barrett, Elizabeth Barrett 40, 159
Baudelaire, Charles 24, 34
Bittner, William xii, 71, 100–1
Blackwood, Algernon 86
Blackwood's Magazine 45, 50
Bliss, Elam 16, 136, 155
Bonaparte, Marie 67
Boston 3, 12
Bransby, Rev. John 6, 7
Broadway Journal 20
Burton, W. E. 66
Burton's Gentleman's Magazine 19, 66, 91

Charleston 13, 72, 84, 98, 101
Charlottesville 10
Chase, Lewis 151
Chesterton, G. K. 97
Clarke, Joseph 9
Clemm, Maria (aunt) 14, 16, 19, 22, 145, 157
Clemm, Virginia *see* Poe, Virginia Clemm
Coleridge, Samuel Taylor 13, 65, 121, 136

Defoe, Daniel 121
Dickens, Charles 18, 32, 40, 76, 93, 108, 137, 157
Doyle, Arthur Conan 86, 90, 93, 97, 100, 115

Eliot, T. S. 164
Emerson, Ralph Waldo 24

Fordham 20
Fort Moultrie *see* Sullivan's Island
Fowles, John 72, 194n.

Galt, William 10
Godwin, William 93
Graham, George R. 25
Graham's Magazine 19, 137
Griswold, Rufus W. 25, 26, 40

Harper & Brothers 49, 119
Hawthorne, Nathaniel 24, 28, 40, 137
Holmes, Sherlock 91, 92, 95
Hopkins, Elizabeth Arnold *see* Poe, Elizabeth Arnold

Irvine 6, 73
Irving, Washington 24, 40, 45

Kafka, Franz 27, 86
Kennedy, John Pendleton 17, 18, 21, 63

Latrobe, J. H. B. 17, 63
Lea & Blanchard 105
London 6, 73, 178

London, Jack 78
Longfellow, Henry Wadsworth 24, 40
Lowell, James Russell 82, 86, 135
Lytton, Bulwer 93

Mackenzie, Mrs William 5
Mallarmé 34
Manor House School 6–7, 73–4
Mason, Monck 130
Melville, Herman 126
Miller, James H. 63
Moore, Thomas 13

New York 7, 15, 19, 20, 129, 144, 157

Orwell, George 27, 32, 109
Osgood, Frances Sargent 55, 56

Paris 91–7, 180
Paulding, J. K. 119
Philadelphia 19, 68
Poe, David (father) 3–4, 22
POE, EDGAR ALLAN
  Themes and Characteristics
  childhood 3–9
  detachment 29
  diversity 29, 111, 147
  divided personality 65, 71–2, 75, 154, 159, 163
  English influences 5–9, 23
  health 21, 83
  literary influences 23–4
  loneliness 27
  narrators 26–7, 32
  pessimism 104–7
  romanticism 26, 31, 165
  science fiction 115–32
  seriousness 26, 28–9

  Works
  Al Aaraaf 13, 38, 154
  Al Aaraaf, Tamerlane and Minor Poems 14, 38, 154–5
  Alone 38, 153–4
  The American Drama 38
  The Angel of the Odd 38
  Annabel Lee 38, 160–1
  The Assignation 38–9

Autography 39
The Balloon-Hoax 39, 129–31
A Bargain Lost *see* Bon-Bon
The Bells 21, 39
Berenice 9, 19, 26, 39
The Black Cat 20, 26–7, 32, 39, 81–2
Bon-Bon 16, 39
Bridal Ballad 41
The Business Man 41
The Cask of Amontillado 21, 27, 32, 33, 41, 88–9
The City in the Sea 41
The Coliseum 41, 62
The Colloquy of Monos and Una 41, 61
The Conchologist's First Book 41
The Conqueror Worm 42
The Conversation of Eiros and Charmion 42
A Descent into the Maelström 30, 42
The Devil in the Belfry 42, 102
Diddling 42, 61, 142–3
Doings of Gotham 42
The Domain of Arnheim 42, 72, 143–5, 171
A Dream 42, 155
Dream-Land 42
Dreams 42
A Dream Within a Dream 43
The Duke de L'Omelette 16, 43
Eldorado 43, 161–4
Eleonora 19, 29, 43
The Elk 43
An Enigma 43
Eulalie 43
Eureka 20, 30, 43, 145–7
Evening Star 43, 165
The Facts in the Case of M. Valdemar 43–4, 86–8, 130
Fairy-Land 44, 155
The Fall of the House of Usher 19, 27, 29, 30, 33, 44, 69–73
A Few Words on Secret Writing 44
For Annie 44
Four Beasts in One 44
The Gold-Bug 13, 19, 27, 29,

Poe, Edgar Allan—*Contd.*
  33, 44, 71, 84, 97–101, 158
  The Happiest Day   44
  The Haunted Palace   44
  Hop-Frog   21, 31, 45, 89–91, 162
  How to Write a Blackwood Article   45
  Hymn   45
  The Imp of the Perverse   32, 45
  The Island of the Fay   45
  Israfel   45
  The Journal of Julius Rodman 45–6, 119
  King Pest   46, 102–4
  The Lake   46
  Landor's Cottage   46, 143
  The Landscape Garden   *see* The Domain of Arnheim
  Lenore   46
  Letter to B——   16, 46, 136–7
  Ligeia   29, 46, 68–9
  The Lighthouse   46
  Lines Written in an Album   46
  Lionising   46
  The Literary Life of Thingum Bob   47
  The Literati   47, 118
  Loss of Breath   16, 47
  Maelzel's Chess Player   47, 91
  The Man of the Crowd   47
  The Man That Was Used Up 47–8
  MS. Found in a Bottle   16, 30, 48, 63–6, 110, 123
  Marginalia   48, 147
  The Masque of the Red Death 29, 33, 48, 76–8
  Mellonta Tauta   48, 61, 109–11
  Mesmeric Revelation   48, 86
  Metzengerstein   16, 48
  Morella   9, 48–9, 66–7
  The Murders in the Rue Morgue   19, 49, 91–3
  The Mystery of Marie Rogêt   30, 49, 62, 93–5
  Mystification   49
  The Narrative of Arthur Gordon Pym   29, 49, 62, 65, 68, 119–29

  Never Bet the Devil Your Head 49
  The Oblong Box   49–50, 83–6
  The Oval Portrait   50, 75–6
  The Philosophy of Composition   50, 62, 140–1
  Philosophy of Furniture   50, 142
  The Pit and the Pendulum   20, 27, 30, 32, 50, 78–81
  Poems   16, 50, 155–7
  The Poetic Principle   50, 141–2
  The Power of Words   50
  A Predicament   50, 102
  The Premature Burial   32, 51, 105
  The Prose Romances of Edgar A. Poe   51
  The Purloined Letter   51, 95–7
  The Rationale of Verse   51
  The Raven   20, 51, 157–9
  The Raven and Other Poems   20, 51
  Rise Infernal Spirits   51
  Romance   51
  Scenes From 'Politian'   51
  Shadow – A Parable   51–2
  Silence – A Fable   52
  The Sleeper   52, 156
  Some Secrets of the Magazine Prison-House   52
  Some Words With a Mummy 52, 104–7, 123
  Sonnet – Silence   52
  Sonnet – To Science   13, 52, 155
  Sonnet – To Zante   52
  The Spectacles   52
  The Sphinx   52
  Spirits of the Dead   52
  Stanzas   52–3
  The System of Doctor Tarr and Professor Fether   53, 107–9
  A Tale of Jerusalem   16, 53, 105
  A Tale of the Ragged Mountains 10, 53
  Tales   20, 53, 111
  Tales of the Folio Club   53–4, 66, 119
  Tales of the Grotesque and Arabesque 19, 54, 61
  Tamerlane   15, 54, 153

Poe, Edgar Allan—*Contd.*
Tamerlane and Other Poems   3, 12, 54, 152–4
The Tell-Tale Heart   20, 26, 32, 54, 82–3
Thou Art The Man   54
The Thousand and Second Tale of Scheherazade   54, 115
Three Sundays in a Week   55
To Helen   9, 55, 156–7
To Isadore   55–6
To My Mother   56
To One in Paradise   56
To the River   56
Ulalume   21, 56, 159–60
The Unparalleled Adventure of One Hans Pfaall   56, 116–8
A Valentine   56
The Valley of Unrest   56
Von Kempelen and his Discovery   56, 161
Why the Little Frenchman Wears his Hand in a Sling   56–7
William Wilson   7, 19, 57, 65, 73–5
X-ing a Paragrab   57
Poe, Elizabeth Arnold (mother)   4–5, 22, 67
Poe, "General" David (grandfather)   4
Poe, Rosalie (sister)   4, 5
Poe, Virginia Clemm (wife)   14, 19, 20, 22, 67, 76, 145, 159, 160–1
Poe, William Henry (brother)   4, 14

Queen, Ellery   97
Quinn, Arthur Hobson   26

Ravenel, Dr Edmund   98
Reynolds, Jeremiah N.   124

Richmond   4, 5, 9, 10, 11, 12, 13, 18–19, 21, 121, 143–4, 173
Richmond, Mrs Nancy   21, 162
Robinson Crusoe   120, 121, 122
Royster, Sarah Elmira   21

Sayers, Dorothy L.   93, 97
Scott, Walter   92
Shaw, Bernard   25
Shelley, Mary   78, 105, 122
Sinclair, David   xii, 23
Southern Literary Messenger   18, 66, 98, 103, 108, 119
Stanard, Jane Stith   9, 14, 22
Stern, Philip Van Doren   xii, 24, 73
Stevenson, R. L.   64, 73, 85, 99, 139–40
Stoke Newington   6–9, 57, 73
Stylus, The   97
Sullivan's Island   13, 98–9, 183

Thomas, Calvin   3, 12
Twain, Mark   104, 137, 194n.

Valentine, Frances Keeling   *see* Allan, Frances Valentine
Verne, Jules   122, 132
Virginia, University of   10

Welles, Orson   130
Wells, H. G.   53, 85–6, 88, 90, 99, 110, 126–9, 130, 139, 194n., 195n.
West Point   14–16
White, Thomas   18, 67
Whitman, Sarah Helen   21, 25, 90
Whitman, Walt   25
Wiley & Putnam   20, 53
Willis, N.   20, 25
Wordsworth, William   136